A

THE GATE OF LIFE

THE GATE OF LIFE

BY

W. R. INGE

DEAN OF ST. PAUL'S, 1911–1934

WITH AN INTRODUCTION BY
THE BISHOP OF LONDON

LONGMANS, GREEN AND CO.
LONDON ✦ NEW YORK ✦ TORONTO

LONGMANS, GREEN AND CO. LTD.
39 PATERNOSTER ROW, LONDON, E.C.4
6 OLD COURT HOUSE STREET, CALCUTTA
53 NICOL ROAD, BOMBAY
36A MOUNT ROAD, MADRAS

LONGMANS, GREEN AND CO.
114 FIFTH AVENUE, NEW YORK
221 EAST 20TH STREET, CHICAGO
88 TREMONT STREET, BOSTON

LONGMANS, GREEN AND CO.
480 UNIVERSITY AVENUE, TORONTO

First published, January, 1935.
Second Impression, January, 1935.

Printed in Great Britain.

INTRODUCTION

THIS book is a parting present from the Dean (as I must still call him for the last time), and I am very grateful to him for again writing one of our Lenten books.

The book was passed on to me by the publisher's reader with the remark that it was " The Dean at his best," and after studying carefully these twelve thoughtful sermons I am inclined to endorse the verdict.

It would be impertinent in me to comment upon the treatment of the vital subjects discussed in these sermons by an author far better known than I am myself, and of course I am not in any way responsible for the opinions expressed in them or for the conclusions drawn, but those who read this volume will find the most vital questions of Life and Death, of Human Suffering, of the Justice of God, of Peace and War, treated with great frankness and reverence by one of the acutest brains in Europe.

I have always wanted our Lenten books, which must now have been issued for thirty years, to be of different kinds and to appeal to different sorts of people, and I heartily commend this book to the many people terribly troubled by the difficulty of reconciling the state of the world as we see it to-day with a belief in the Power and Love of an Almighty God.

A. F. LONDON:

PREFACE

THE Addresses in this little book were written long before the formal farewell to my public which was published in September, 1934, under the title *Vale*. They have been collected in response to the kind request of the Bishop of London, that I would for the second time write the devotional book for Lent which appears every year with a Preface by himself. It will be seen that most of the Addresses were intended in the first instance for University students, but I hope that others also may find them helpful.

W. R. INGE.

BRIGHTWELL MANOR,
  WALLINGFORD.

CONTENTS

" Except a corn of wheat fall into the ground and die, it abideth alone."—St. John xii. 24.

" Blessed is he that shall eat bread in the Kingdom of God."
—St. Luke xiv. 15.
" The Kingdom of God is not eating and drinking, but righteousness and peace and joy in the Holy Ghost."—Rom. xiv. 37.

" When the Son of Man cometh, shall He find faith on the earth."
—St. Luke xviii. 8.

" If in this life only we have hope in Christ, we are of all men most miserable."—1 Cor. xv. 19.

" Ye have not passed this way heretofore."—Joshua iii. 4.

" For their sakes I consecrate myself."—St. John, xvii. 19.

" Every man that setteth up his idols in his heart, I the Lord will answer him according to the multitude of his idols."
—Ezek. xiv. 4.

" He taught them many things by parables."—St. Mark iv. 2.

CONTENTS

CHAPTER I

DEATH THE GATE OF LIFE

"EXCEPT a corn of wheat fall into the ground and die, it abideth alone." The universal and inexorable doom of all life is here pronounced by Him Who abolished death. Jesus Christ abolished death in the only way in which a stubborn fact can be abolished—by showing that it is not what it appears to be. Death appears to be the seal of failure, it is the condition of success ; it appears to be an end, it is also a beginning ; it appears to be a humiliation and a curse, but its cleansing waters purge the soul of her travel-stains, and land her refreshed upon the farther shore. Death, says the Book of Genesis, is a punishment. Death, says science, is no punishment, but a law of Nature. Death, says Jesus Christ, is nothing save the gate through which one passes into immortal life. Death is a punishment if we will have it so. If we turn into ends what were meant to be instruments ; if we use that wonderful idealising power which belongs to us to give a false and spurious substance to fleeting shadows whose nature it is to come and go, and to desires which, so idealised and intensified, can never be satisfied, then death, which dissolves these cloud-palaces into thin air, will be to us a punishment—a punishment for mistaking shadow for substance, and attempting to slake the divine thirst of the soul in the waters of a mirage.

Death is a law, if we will have it so. The rhythm of reproduction and dissolution, of growth and decay, may seem to swing evenly backwards and forwards. The study of Nature may, and probably will, lead us only to the manly resignation of Marcus Aurelius, and to the Stoic's resolve to steel the heart against emotions which tend to discontent or rebellion against Nature's laws. " Depart, then, satisfied, since He Who releases thee is satisfied." Very many have tried to be content with this courageous submission, and to " cut down long hopes within a narrow compass."

And yet, if we will have it so, death is the gate of life. What was the secret, the hidden source, of St. Paul's joyous attitude towards the thought of death ? Why did he look forward to "finish his course with joy ", instead of only to "depart satisfied " ? What made him so sure that " to die is gain " ? His belief in the Resurrection, of course. But this belief rested not only on what he saw in the clouds on the road to Damascus, not only on the reports of the Twelve and the survivors of the " five hundred brethren " who had seen the risen Christ, but on the overpowering conviction, to which the Resurrection of Christ opened his eyes, that death has no sting to those who know the hidden laws of life. The passage from death unto life is no unique portent ; it is the open secret of the universe, which Jesus Christ brought to light. In the world without it is exemplified in every harvest-field. " That which thou sowest is not quickened except it die." The seed " dies " ; it does not perish entirely, else the analogy would fail ; but it dies as a seed, and takes new life as a blade. In the world within St. Paul knew what it was to die to the old man, to die and be buried with Christ, and to rise again into newness of life.

Is this analogy from Nature really valid and helpful ? Many have doubted it. To some the law of renewal in Nature has seemed only to make the fate of mankind more cruel by contrast. The well-known lines of Catullus have had many echoes in literature. And if an impartial view of Nature, including man, does give us something immortal, namely, the law of mortality, and something invariable, namely, the law of change, is this much comfort to us ?

St. Paul's analogy, like most appeals to external Nature made by religious teachers, is rather poetical than scientific. We cannot remain on purely scientific grounds when we are dealing with religion, because religion is concerned not only with existence, but with values. When we look at the ceaseless flux of Nature from this point of view, some new considerations suggest themselves. If there is no final upward movement for any living thing, but only a curve ending on the same plane as the starting-point ; if all nature is simply a repetition of the same processes, a series of revolutions of the same machinery, then the time-process has no value and no meaning at all. Nay, it would be worse than meaningless—it would be foolishness. For endless repetition stales and spoils everything. Such a world would be an irrational world. And an irrational world, with even one rational creature condemned to inhabit it, would be an evil world. However, so far as we know, there is no such thing as unending repetition in Nature. The planets are cooling. The sun is cooling, though recent discoveries give him a longer life than was formerly believed. The doom of death hangs over the immeasurably great as well as over the immeasurably small. There is only one way in which the values of life can escape the doom of the existences to which they are linked ; and that is by constant transmutation into values of a higher quality. Cling to them as they are, and they fade and perish ; let them go, make a living sacrifice of them, and they will still be yours, transmuted and enhanced. That which we receive in exchange for what we have given up is never the same as what we surrendered. In St. Paul's words, " Thou sowest not that body which shall be, but bare grain." The new life is always life on another plane. And if we make a living sacrifice of ourselves in reasonable service to God, the new man whom we shall put on in return for the old man whom we have put off is not just our old selves back again, but a new self, nearer to the image of God.

This mysterious law of the spiritual world, the law of death and re-birth as the condition of all growth and all permanence, has been dimly perceived by nearly all religions. The more we study the dogmas, the ritual, and the sacred mysteries of the various religions that have flourished among men (excluding the worship of mere savages), the more impressed we shall be by the universality of symbolism intended to express the law of spiritual death and re-birth. If there be a " key to all mythologies " it is here. Men have felt that everywhere in Nature God has stamped some hint of the law of re-birth. The changing seasons, the rising and setting suns, the time-process itself, with its mysterious register, human memory—all point to the central law of the higher life, " That which thou sowest is not quickened, except it die." This train of thought has its value as an argument for our survival after death. It is, indeed, the chief foundation of our faith in a future life. Without undervaluing the argument from divine justice, which is not satisfied, so far as we can see, by the distribution of rewards and punishments in this world ; without undervaluing the confident claim of human love, which asserts its prerogative as the most divine part of our nature, to insist that it has the quality of everlastingness, so that neither death nor life nor any other creature can separate us from love, whether human or divine, or terminate our capacities of loving and being loved—without undervaluing these arguments, I still think that the strongest argument for immortality is the unquenchable conviction that in the mind of God values are facts, and indestructible facts. Whatever has value in God's sight is safe for evermore ; time and change cannot touch it. And so far as we can make our own those things which we know to be precious in His eyes, we have the assurance that for us too death has no importance, save as the entrance to another state, in which those same treasures will be ours, purer and more unalloyed.

But the law of re-birth has also an intimate bearing on our daily life. It should determine our whole attitude towards our experience. What did St. Paul mean by saying, " I die daily " ? Did he simply mean that he was in constant peril of death ? No ; his words have a much deeper meaning. They mean that the law of sacrifice has become a constant part of his experience. He is conscious that deaths and re-births are continually going on within him. His whole life has taught him that all gain comes through pain, all profit through loss. He began, it may be, with a hard struggle against his lower appetites. At least, the lurid picture of the internecine warfare between flesh and spirit, too strongly painted to represent the average experience, must surely have been drawn from his own spiritual combat ; and we know that such highly-strung, neurotic temperaments as his have often to pass through the fire in this way. Then there came the call to surrender the pride of legal righteousness, and the treasure, too highly valued, of Rabbinical learning. All that he had counted gain was now to be set down as loss, yea, counted but as refuse, that he might win Christ. Henceforth he walked the earth as one already dead, and yet continually dying anew—always bearing about with him the dying of the Lord Jesus, that the life of the Lord Jesus might be made manifest in him. Yes, he knew, more intimately than it is given to most of us to know it, that it is the nature of all earthly things, either to perish and be lost, or to be transmuted into values of a higher quality. The new life is never the same as the old. Instruments are used up in realising ends, and lower ends become instruments for realising higher ends.

Is not this the deeper meaning of the tragic *catharsis*, the purgation of the emotions of pity and fear, which Aristotle tells us is the psychological basis of the pleasure which we experience in witnessing a fine tragedy ? The pleasure is not, as he seems to think, self-regarding. It is rather that we love to see a noble and moving representation of the great law of sacrifice, the source of all human tears, but also of the deepest human joys. No pure hopes are ever either gratified or frustrated. The great ones of the earth, the elect spirits, have all died in faith, not having received the promise. God has provided some better thing for them, and for the cause for which they laboured. They lament not now, if they ever did lament, that they have laboured in vain, and spent their strength for nought. Their hopes are more than fulfilled, even in being baffled :—

The high that proved too high, the heroic for earth too hard,
　The passion that left the ground to lose itself in the sky,
Are music sent up to God by the lover and the bard :
　Enough that he heard it once ; we shall hear it by and by.

And what is our failure here but a triumph's evidence
　For the fulness of the days ? Have we withered or agonised ?
Why else was the pause prolonged but that singing might issue
　　thence ?
　Why rushed the discords in, but that harmony should be prized ?

It is therefore our wisdom to live with this thought of gain through loss always before our minds. And then, when the last sacrifice is demanded of us—the sacrifice of our lives—we shall find it easy to trust death to do for us what the daily dyings of life have always done for us—to take away much and to give us more, to deprive us of earth that it may give us heaven.

I do not think that we ought to dwell much on the thought of death ; indeed, I am not sure that Spinoza was wrong when he said that there is no subject on which the " free " man will ponder less often than on his own death. One of the most illuminating thinkers among our contemporaries was accustomed to say " Death does not count." It does not count, in this sense—that it is not of great moment whether God calls us in youth, middle age, or old age. God is just and merciful, and will somehow give us all a fair chance of doing and being what He requires of us. We need not trouble ourselves about the fate of unbaptised infants, or persons cut off, as it seems to us, without the opportunity of preparing for death. We are much more sure that God is just than that " as the tree falls so must it lie." I rejoice, too, that the rather vulgar and morbid attitude towards death which was common in the last century is now felt to be in bad taste. And I hope that we are losing, together with the fashion of parading our bereavements, that disinclination to talk and think about the dead which is the obverse side of the same false sentiment. Let us do all in our power to " keep the memory green " of those whom we have loved and lost, and not behave as if some tragic or shameful thing had befallen them or us.

If we could face the changes and chances of this mortal life in the simple faith that they are meant to be stepping-stones, and not stumbling-blocks ; if we could face them with a fixed resolve to tear the heart of goodness out of what appears to us as evil, confident that all things must work together for good to those who love God, how much useless friction and fretting we should escape, and how much braver and happier our lives would be ! This is the secret of Christian optimism, which makes it so different from the shallow kinds of optimism which offer in vain to " heal slightly " the wounds of life. Christianity shirks nothing, ignores nothing. It does not starve the emotions in the hope of becoming invulnerable. That last act of cowardice, which makes Stoicism false to itself, it renounces. It rejoices heartily with those that rejoice, and weeps sincerely with those that weep. It does not class the purest earthly joys and the tenderest earthly sorrows as things indifferent. It is not ashamed to feel, and to feel deeply. But it finds a heart of joy in the midst of sorrow. It is able even to glory in weakness and tribulation, as the appointed birth-pangs of a richer life. It combats and overcomes temporal evils, not by refusing to recognise them, but by transmuting them. It teaches us, in a word, that all values are permanent, but that all, in so far as they are linked with time and change, must die in order that they may live for ever.

CHAPTER II

THE KINGDOM OF GOD

THE earliest Christianity regarded the Ascension as the penultimate scene of a drama which was very shortly to have its *dénouement* by the reappearance of the Messiah on the clouds of heaven. This is a fact which, however unwelcome it may be to us, we ought, no doubt, to face ; and recent critics of Christianity are determined that we shall face it, with all that follows from it. It is the storm-centre of Christian apologetics at the present time.

Nothing but our uncritical manner of studying Holy Scripture could have hidden from us so long the double thread which runs, entangled but not united, through the New Testament. On the one side we have the whole scheme of salvation presented to us under the forms of time and place : the place, Judæa, the time, the generation of men then living. The method of God's final interposition is conceived of as external, sudden, violent, wholly miraculous. It is bound up, it would seem, with the beliefs that the earth is, as it were, the first floor of a three-storied building ; that Jerusalem is the centre of the earth, and that the end of all things is at hand. On the other side we have the ideas of Christ as the Head of the Church, of a Kingdom in this world but not of this world ; of the indwelling Spirit of Christ as the guiding star of the divine society during its probation as a Church militant ; of Christian practice as a distinctive ethical rule, based on the counsels and example of the Founder ; and of salvation as the attainment of eternal life—that is to say of a higher state of existence, " beyond this bourne of time and place," a blessed state to be fully realised in the future, but which in a measure may be ours on earth.

The Christianity of the New Testament, we are now told, began as a religion of the former type, and ended as a religion of the latter type. All through St. Paul's epistles we can trace the gradual evanescence of the crude Messianic belief, and the approximation to the spiritual religion which we find in the Epistle to the Hebrews, and in a still more advanced form in the Fourth Gospel. There is (it is admitted by all) abundant justification for a spiritualised eschatology between the covers of the New Testament. But the question which now presses upon us is whether this kind of Christianity, which is the religion of most of us, can claim the authority of Jesus Christ Himself. There is a school of critics who would have us believe that Jesus never contemplated founding a Church or instituting a rule of life for future generations; that His one message was that the Kingdom of heaven is at hand, or in modern language that the world is coming to an end. He went about, we are told, warning His countrymen of an impending catastrophe, in which all existing conditions would be subverted, and a supernatural Messianic reign established.

I need not dwell upon the destructive character of this theory. It is enough to say that since the alleged predictions were falsified in every particular, and since outside these predictions we are allowed by these critics to claim very little as the authentic teaching of our Lord, Christianity, as based on the incarnation of the Son of God in the person of the historical Jesus Christ, is torn up by the roots. It appears that there are some Christians, both Roman Catholics and Protestants, who do not regard this treatment of our Saviour as intolerable; I confess that I can neither agree with their arguments nor understand their position. After carefully reading Schweitzer's portrait of the Founder of Christianity, I cannot see that the figure there portrayed has any claim to the reverence, or even the respect, of the world.

On the other hand, the view hitherto commonly held by most Christians, that our Lord promised to return to earth at a far distant date unknown to Himself, does not seem to have any support in the New Testament. The day and the hour, we read, were unknown ; but the predictions, as they stand in our documents, clearly assert that the return, or coming, of the Son of man was imminent. We are not therefore justified, it seems to me, in claiming that we can escape the difficulty by the supposition that the disciples simply antedated the fulfil-ment of a prophecy which still holds good.

Criticism has also, I believe, finally disposed of the view that the Christ of the Synoptics is a purely human teacher of righteousness. Even in St. Mark the portrait is quite clearly that of a man who was not as other men are. Dr. Hatch has said that between the Sermon on the Mount and the Nicene Creed we pass from a world of Syrian peasants to a world of Greek philosophers. The truth is that what he chooses to call Greek metaphysics is either implicit or explicit in the earliest books of the New Testament, the Epistles of St. Paul.

If these paths out of the maze are closed, what shall we do ? Our Lord is recorded in the Gospels to have made predictions which certainly have not been, and cannot now be fulfilled, predictions moreover which, if they were an essential part of His message, must have profoundly modified the whole of His practical teaching, making it only suited to the brief interval before the end of all things should come. Let us face this difficulty, and consider it mainly from the psychological side, for I think the solution must be found in this region.

Christianity began with the teaching of John the Baptist, who, as far as we can make out, preached a *moral* preparation for a *supernatural* catastrophe. Because the two were not brought into vital connexion, his preaching was stern and terrifying. It was like the visions of judgment which have often been unfolded to trembling listeners by Christian preachers.

Our Lord was understood to use much the same language about the need of repentance and the imminence of judgment; but, by bringing the two into vital connexion in His doctrine of the Fatherhood of God, he changed the dynamic of religion from fear and awe to hope and love, and also modified both conceptions to an extent which gradually became apparent. For the repentance which is the first stage of loving, filial obedience fears no celestial thunderbolts, and the kingdom which the Father of our Lord Jesus Christ had prepared for His children could not be ushered in by any Jewish apocalypse. Messianism was shattered from within; only the husk remained. The disciples did not see this at first; they were only conscious that something overwhelming was happening among them. Their minds were filled with a great hope—a dazzling blinding hope which only grew stronger after the tragic end of the earthly mission. It was revealed to them that their Master was not dead but alive; they knew that He had not deserted them. They felt the kingdom of God creating itself in their hearts— a kingdom which was still an idea and not an outward institution, " the liquid ore, as it were, melted by the heavenly flame but not yet cast into the mould."[1] They felt that they were living not amid the anticipations of prophecy, but in the hour of its fulfilment. Past and future were almost blotted out in the vivid reality of the present. In such states of spiritual exaltation men take the current conceptions of the unseen world and pour a new spirit into them. They use the common language, but assuredly not in the common sense of the words.

[1] Jowett, St. Paul's Epp. i. 56.

When a man is possessed by the Spirit of God, and feels all heaven within him, he may use the language of his childhood about the gold and jewels of heaven's streets, and the winged messengers of the King, but assuredly his faith is not childish or materialistic; it belongs to a different class altogether.

When we are asked to believe that the faith of the first Christians consisted solely of crude apocalyptic dreams, which our Saviour taught them, we have a right to claim that the tree be judged by its fruits. Was early Christianity a religion of this kind, or was it a religion of a totally different kind?

We know the apocalyptic type of religion; it is a real type; it exists. Its normal results are either political insurgence or selfish quietism; in either case indifference to social morality; neglect of duties; nervous excitement; and rapid evanescence. There was, naturally enough, a flicker of this sort of primitive anabaptism in early Christianity, as we see from the strictures in St. Paul's earlier epistles; but will anyone maintain that the true follower of Christ is the man who in his most religious moments speaks with tongues and behaves as if he was drunk? Consider the calm, unemotional character of all our Lord's preaching. What are His great antitheses? Not between the present world and the millennium, but between God and Mammon, sincerity and hypocrisy, love and hatred. Consider how conspicuously absent are any descriptions of the state of the blessed in the " kingdom of God." Compare the Gospels with the Revelation of St. John, and with contemporary apocalyptic literature, and note the vast difference. If there are a few passages in our Gospels which might serve to flatter the fond hopes of the disciples that such a return as they expected was near, is it not extremely likely that they are coloured by the pathetic longing—so very natural in the circumstances—to see their Lord vindicated as the Son of God before the eyes of the world? Very few critics accept as authentic the apocalyptic prophecy in Mark xiii ; may there not be one or two more innocent interpolations of the same kind ?

I do not wish entirely to exclude the possibility that our Lord, in becoming man, may have been willing to share, to some extent, the current popular illusions, both with regard to the Messianic hope, and demoniacal possession. But this must certainly not be stretched so far as to admit that He fancied himself filling the rôle of Daniel's Son of Man in the near future. Such a notion would not be compatible with sanity, far less with those attributes which all Christians believe Him to have possessed. What the disciples thought about Him is another matter. It may be laid down as a rule that a conversion always begins with a misunderstanding. We are attracted in the first instance not by the reality, but by some preconceived idea of our own, which drops off as we come to know the reality. Messianism in point of fact dropped off very early from Christianity, like a protecting shell which was no longer needed. It dropped off with hardly any convulsion. Not so very long after Christians ceased to pray " come, Lord Jesus," they began to pray *pro mora finis*—that the end might not come just yet.

One difficulty, however, remains. Why, it may be asked, if the first Christians believed—I will not say the crudities attributed to them by some modern writers, but what St. Paul believed when he wrote 1 Thessalonians, did they take the trouble to collect, preserve, and commit to writing the records of our Lord's life and ministry ? Why did they embark on the immense task of converting the Roman Empire ? Why did they organise Churches ? And lastly, when they found that no Messiah was to be expected from the clouds, why did they continue to believe in, and to spread, a religion which had so grievously belied their hopes ?

The answer must be sought, I think, in the peculiar nature of eschatological beliefs. If we examine our own ideas about the future life—compounded as they are of theories about the resurrection of the body and the immortality of the soul, about the New Jerusalem and the sphere of eternal realities, about possible further probation, final reward, and final punishment, we shall have to admit that our eschatology is a tangled mass of contradictory theories, such as we should find quite intolerable if any other subject was under discussion. We do not find it intolerable, because we do not really believe in these pictures of the world beyond the grave in the same way in which we believe facts of experience. We know that we are immortal, and that our eternal happiness or misery is somehow determined by our conduct. All beyond this is quite vague ; we form images which we know to be inadequate, and these images have so little body that we do not mind if they clash with each other—as our attempts to envisage the eternal world under the forms of time, of space, and of substance, certainly do. With all our vivid pictures of heaven and hell, we know that eye hath not seen, nor ear heard, neither hath it entered into the heart of man to conceive, even the fringes of the truth about these things. "*Nescio, nescio, quae iubilatio*" must be our last word on these mysteries.

It is a very superficial view, that any religion is based upon its eschatology. This is never, I believe, the root of a creed, but always its flower or its fruit. It could never give birth to religious faith, for belief in human survival in time, or in the approaching end of the world, has in itself nothing to do with religion. Besides, no one would believe that the world was coming to an end, or that the dead shall rise, because someone told him ; it is absurd to suppose such a thing. These beliefs are always the product of a lively faith, kindled quite otherwise. Fitzgerald was not far wrong when he said that heaven is but the vision of fulfilled desire, and hell the shadow from a soul on fire. It was the intensity of Christian faith and hope that

first created and then transmuted the dream of the return of
Jesus upon the clouds. Jewish thought always envisaged the
divine under the form of time, and dynamically. But just
because these beliefs are the reflection of the soul's deepest intuitions, their substance is felt to be independent of their form
to a degree wholly unique. The spirit quickeneth; the flesh
profiteth nothing. And so, though the early Christians
thought they believed in the approaching end of the age, they
did not behave as if they really believed it; and when the
Kingdom of God changed into the ideal of a Christian Church,
the second coming into the gift of the Holy Spirit, and the
passing away of the earth into the passing away of each individual in turn from the earth, they were conscious of no shock,
and in fact found that the teaching of Christ was much better
adapted to the new belief than the old. The new wine of
Christianity burst the wine-skins of Messianism in a very short
time; but no wine was lost; the treasure was transferred to
other vessels.

If these considerations are right, it is utterly impossible that
our Lord's teaching can have been "purely eschatological."
The "pure eschatologist" is only to be found in a lunatic
asylum, and I doubt whether he would have been taken much
more seriously in Judæa than in London. And therewith goes
the dismal verdict that the historical Jesus is to us a stranger
and an alien (*ein Fremdling*). To seek the essence of a great
revelation in the transitory links which connect it with the
superstitions of the age is a most perverse proceeding; it is
like saying that the only important part of a building is the
scaffolding. Every great man is linked to his own generation by
his weakest side, and his contemporaries sometimes make the
most of what is least significant in his message. We cannot
admit that there was any weaker side in our divine Master;
but there was a point of attachment to His own generation, and,

so far, the law holds good. The character of Christ and the
nature of His teaching are surely very well known to us. He
was not a modern European, certainly and fortunately ; but
neither was he a typical Syrian peasant. It is safe to say that
no one who has tried to imitate Christ has found Him hard to
understand ; hard to follow, no doubt, not because He is a
stranger and an alien to us, but because He is so far above us,
and because we are strangers and aliens to our true selves.

Therefore I do not think that this latest attack upon the
historical Christ has any chance of success, though it will, I fear,
cause much distress if it is popularised. But let us make no
mistake about the character of this theory. It is an attack upon
Christianity itself. Christianity is and always has been a religion of devotion to a real Person. This is its *differentia*. It
belongs definitely to this type of religion ; and you cannot
change the type of a religion without destroying it. If you
separate Christianity from the historical Christ, you will get
one of three results. Either the thinly-disguised Paganism of
Southern Europe, or the deliberate sophistication which keeps
idealism in reserve for the educated, and trades on the superstitions of the vulgar ; or a pure mysticism which has no connexion with history. As for those who would retain eviscerated
dogmas as practically edifying, one may fairly ask these religious pragmatists for whom this treatment is intended. The
man of simple faith may be trusted to express himself very
forcibly as soon as he understands what his teacher means by
" representative truth." The man of the world will pass a
swift and scornful judgment upon the Christian minister who,
as he would roughly but not unfairly put it, no longer believes
in Jesus Christ. The expedient seems to be acceptable only
to the small class of sceptics who wish to remain Churchmen.
It would be deplorable if we were to throw away all that
devout Liberal scholarship has done, especially in Germany,

to elucidate the character and teaching of our Blessed Lord. Inadequate as it must appear to Churchmen, it is of inestimable value as far as it goes. It has given us a faithful picture of the historical Christ as our perfect Teacher and our perfect Example. It has shown us, far more clearly than we saw before, that the real source of Christian faith was the profound and wholly unique impression which the personality of our Blessed Lord made upon those who saw and heard Him. Let us build upon this foundation, and go as much further as we will. Can we not hear His voice saying "Will ye also go away?" And shall we not answer, "Lord, to whom shall we go? Thou hast the words of eternal life."

CHAPTER III

THE CHURCH AND THE WORLD

WITHIN recent times three or four writers have won a brief notoriety by imaginary descriptions of a return of Christ in human form to one of the centres of civilisation —to Chicago, or London, or Paris. One attempt of the kind, a book called *Il est ressuscité*, is said to have had a large sale in France. The piquancy of such books consists partly, no doubt, in pointing out how little there is of real Christianity in the lives of professing Christians—the clergy, for example ; but partly also in a naïve surprise that after so many centuries of Christianity the world should still be the world—a power ranged as an enemy against those who wish to lead the higher life. In short, we are accustomed to think of our civilisation as Christian, till some one shows us that it is nothing of the kind.

The world—that is, human society as it organises itself for social purposes—is still unconverted. At other times, Christians would have said, So much the worse for the world. But that, it seems, is now regarded as blasphemy against the democratic principle, against what Defoe calls "the lady Majority, the infallible decider of cases known and unknown, the great Pope Joan of the age." Instead of the world being on its trial before the saints, as St. Paul imagined, we now see Christianity arraigned, tried, and condemned on the heinous charge of "appealing to the few." *Plebecula locuta est ; causa finita est.* We are also told that the majority lose nothing in rejecting Christianity, because in the Middle Ages, when everyone believed, Europe was wickeder than it is now. Writers like Cotter Morison have no difficulty in proving that morality in the so-called Ages of Faith was shockingly bad. But instead of drawing the true conclusion that then, as now, real Christians were in a small minority, and that conformity, at a time when heresy sent people to the stake, had no necessary connexion with real conviction, he argues that Christianity has been proved to have no influence upon conduct. The same idea seems to trouble some recent apologists, who have tried to account for the apparent failure of Christianity, the apparent failure, in their eyes, being shown not so much by looseness of conduct, as by the fact that, while the disinherited classes are becoming impatient for a fairer distribution of the good things of the world, the Church has no sword ready to cut that most intricate of Gordian knots. Strange as it must seem to any thoughtful reader of the New Testament, many Christians are seriously uneasy at finding the Church numerically so weak ; it seems to them an indication that something must be wrong with our religion. Even our leaders sometimes adopt an apologetic and deprecating tone which is quite unnecessary, and hardly dignified in the holders of a divine commission. We cannot fail to see everywhere signs of discouragement.

Worse than discouragement are the attempts made to adulterate our message to suit the popular taste. This faithless and impatient policy takes two forms, which of course may be and often are combined. Many of our clergy rush in, where wiser men would fear to tread, into the labyrinth of the social question, a task for which they are unprepared by any serious study of economics and political philosophy. Their ignorant tirades do almost unmixed harm, by confusing the issues and exciting passion ; nor should we forget the injustice done to employers of labour by denouncing them as a class for cupidity and callousness. All honour to those who are willing in person to share the life of the poor ; that is a social service which our Master approved by example and precept. But agitation is not the business of the Church. Our duty is to hold up steadily the Christian standard of values, and to show that we ourselves accept it. It is the prevalence of a false standard of values, among rich and poor alike, that has created the problem, and that makes it at present insoluble. There lies our task, and not in persuading the working-man that we are on his side in every industrial dispute.

The second fruit of impatience and faithlessness appears in what has been euphemistically called the study of human needs in religion. An educated man, who mixes much with average men and women of any class, will soon find what a very thin layer of culture is often spread over the crude mental processes of the essential barbarian. People crave for permission to indulge their primitive taste for marvels, magic, spiritism, and all the accessories of the lower religions. The mental habits of thousands of years have not been eradicated by a superficial education. It is possible to gain an apparent success by what is really an act of treason against the spirit of progress, by exploiting those " human needs " which civilised people are growing ashamed of, though they still feel them. The average person wants something less austerely moral, less intellectual, more exciting and amusing, than the Gospel of Christ. Shall we gratify these " human needs " or no ? Cannot we distinguish between those helps to worship which are really elevating, such as dignified ceremonial and beautiful music, which, at least in our great cathedrals, should be used freely to make worship as stately and noble as possible, and that kind of " revival " which should be called a reversion ? The final fate of Greek philosophy should be a warning to us. That noble ship in her last voyage took on board such a load of theosophy,

C

theurgy, and magic, that she foundered with her cargo. The same fate awaits any Church which deliberately trades on the superstitions of the vulgar. That policy involves progressive degeneration ; the transition from accommodation to deception is very easy, and the clientèle who have to be catered for becomes more and more debased. In the long run, the only true policy is to give the people the best and highest that we know, whether they will hear or whether they will forbear.

The words of Christ, " When the Son of Man cometh, shall he find faith (or the faith) upon the earth ? " which sound so gloomy that many have doubted their authenticity, are a severe rebuke to any anxiety for rapid success. Our Lord seems to contemplate calmly what the world would call the final failure of His redemptive work. He is rejected in His lifetime by a sinful generation, and His disciples will fare no better. " If they have called the master of the house Beelzebub, how much more them of his household ? If they have persecuted me, they will also persecute you." And this state of warfare against heavy odds is to continue to the end. " When the Son of Man cometh, shall he find faith on the earth ? " With His Divine insight He even foresaw the sad victory of a World-Church, a theocratic empire no longer directed by His ideals or made up of His disciples. " Not everyone that saith unto me Lord, Lord, shall enter into the kingdom of heaven, but he that doeth the will of my Father which is in heaven.' If palpable, blatant success is the blessing of the Old Testament, it certainly is not the promise of the New.

It was in the third century that the Church began deliberately to compete with other popular religions for the dominion of the world. In that period we find it incorporating elements which were the common property of all the chief cults in the Roman Empire. It is true that Christian worship remained clean, and eschewed necromancy and bloody sacrifices; but in other respects the State-religion of Constantine and his successors was the most comprehensive of all the rival syncretisms. Paganism was exterminated in the fourth and fifth centuries with a thoroughness which left the spasmodic and half-hearted attempts at persecution by the Pagan emperors far behind; but there were few Pagan martyrs, since the respectable "Hellene" who accepted Christianity was not required to abandon anything that he cared much about except his beautiful statues. The *nomina* rather than the *numina* of his worship were changed. From that time to this there has been no sort of correspondence between Church membership and real Christianity. The Church has been obviously a *corpus mixtum*. From time to time revolts against this state of things have occurred, and men have advocated the Puritan ideal, that the Church should consist only of those who earnestly desire to lead the Christian life. But the Parables of the Tares, and of the Drag-net, seem to sanction the Catholic theory, that the Church on earth should contain all sorts, bad and good. The mischief arises when, after accepting the necessity of an institutional Church of wheat and tares, we proceed to identify it collectively with the Body of Christ, which is the ideal or eternal Church, the whole body in heaven and earth named after Christ. It is the illegitimate combination of these two views which has led to persecution, fraudulent or forcible conversions, and other evils.

The true history of Christ's religion is in the biographies of the saints. The saints are the runners in the sacred torch-race, handing on the flame which was lighted in Palestine nineteen hundred years ago, and which by God's grace shall never be put out. These true disciples of Christ have never been very numerous. There has never been any inconvenient crowd at the narrow gate. In every generation many are called, but few chosen. It follows that if we are real Christians, we must expect to find ourselves in a small minority. Ours will never be the religion either of the classes or of the masses. As Bishop Edward Talbot once said, " Nothing in Scripture and little in experience would lead us to think that the majority in any class, time or place, will make Christian faith and principles their own."

It is, then, easy to prove that " the apparent failure of Christianity " was foreseen by its Founder. But a more formidable question will next be raised, " Why is the Christian type of character so rare ? " It is a favourite method of courteously dismissing the claims of Christianity, to say, " I quite recognise that Christian saintliness is a delicate and beautiful thing ; the world would be much poorer without it. But it is a natural endowment, and a rare one, like musical or poetical genius. I have it not, and therefore it is useless for me to try for it." Well, the answer to that is that the enjoyment of music and poetry is not confined to those who can themselves produce masterpieces, and that a man need not give up the practice of Christianity because he is not likely to be a St. Francis. If we are asked why the higher qualities of religious genius are so rare, I do not see that we can be expected to answer the question. Racial development is very slow, at least if we take the duration of an individual life as the unit. A biologist or geologist, who is at home in calculations of time involving millions of years, would not consider two thousand years a long period in the history of our race, nor would he expect that the revelation of a possible new birth into a diviner life—life on a higher plane of existence—which was made "in the fullness of time", that is to say at the earliest possible moment, by the Incarnation of our Lord, should have made any great changes in average human nature in about sixty generations. If we can trace some moral and spiritual progress, and surely we can, it is as much as we have a right to expect.

I am assuming that what the Incarnation of the Son of God brought us is, first and foremost, the new birth into a new life ——the life of the Spirit. This new life is characterised by a more vivid consciousness of God's presence, of His personal care and fatherly love ; by a more spontaneous recourse to prayer, intercession, and thanksgiving ; by a joyous confidence that all things must work together for good to those who love God ; by ready affection and sympathy to our fellows ; by freedom from anxiety about the changes and chances of life ; by a strong sense of duty, and genuine sorrow and shame for our sins ; lastly by an almost lighthearted indifference to death, based on a conviction that no power in earth or heaven can separate us from the love of God, which is in Christ Jesus our Lord.

This is a type of character which we all know and honour. We have all met a few real Christians. And is it not probable that those who seem to us to live on a higher plane than other men, to be in correspondence with a higher order of reality than that of which others are conscious, are as it were the harbingers of an upward step in human evolution, which at present only appears sporadically, and, like other new acquisitions, has a precarious struggle for survival ? Certainly the language of the New Testament about the old and new man, about the higher self, the Christ-life, which takes the place of the old lower self, lends itself very easily to the notion that with the coming of Christ a "new creation", a permanent enhancement of the spiritual endowments of humanity, made its first appearance in the world.

We Churchmen must be on our guard against identifying the " new creation in Christ Jesus " with what has been called " devotionality." Our Lord, in point of fact, did not choose his Apostles from men of that type. Tax-collectors and fishermen are not generally religious mystics, and indeed the Apostles do not seem to have been what we should call religiously gifted at all. Perhaps no one but Christ would have seen what was in them, or would have composed his little band of such materials. I have said that the Christian type is recognisable ; but perhaps there is no sure test except " By their fruits ye shall know them." It is a common snare for the clergy to mistake devotionality for the goodness which God values. Just as the schoolmaster, in proportion to his weakness as a disciplinarian, likes and favours the obedient boy who sits still and does not break rules, so the clergyman, in proportion to his ineffectiveness as a fisher of men, admires and loves the docile and regular churchgoer, who sits at the feet of the vicar for the time being. Christ, at any rate, chose to make heroes and martyrs out of typical laymen. He saw the most glorious possibilities in an apparently commonplace character, just as He saw germs of hope and health in apparently incurable human wrecks. This is an aspect of genuine Christianity which has been recovered, I might almost say, in our time, and largely through the poetry of Robert Browning. He is never so happy as when he is showing us that there is a soul of goodness in things evil, an unquenched spark of the divine fire in the veriest rascal. We shall find these scattered germs of noble promise in many unexpected places, if we look for them.

But though manifestations of human goodness meet us everywhere, and would be more apparent to us than they are if we were better men ourselves, it remains true that the world is still the world, still unconverted, still hostile to Christ. It is surely true—though it sounds like a bald and harsh statement—that while Christ was an optimist about individuals, He was almost a pessimist about organised society. He knew that when men act collectively, as a mob, or a party, they are apt to behave worse than they would dream of doing as individuals. The irresponsibility of a gang seems to vary directly with its size. Christ prayed for His murderers, but He "prayed not for the world", that is to say, for organised society. And every human association is in danger of becoming a little "world." We are not warned half often enough of the moral dangers of that *esprit de corps*, the good side of which is so constantly, and justly, commended to us.

It seems plain, from the whole tenor of Christ's teaching, that the Church is to save the world by being unlike it. The metaphors of the salt, the leaven, the candlestick, the city set on a hill, all point this way. It is the slowest of all methods, but then God is not pressed for time. As the German proverb says, He does not make up His accounts every Saturday. If we believe in immortality we can acquiesce in the very unshowy work which is given us to do, and we shall save those who come after us the trouble of clearing away the ambitious buildings which perhaps we should like to erect from our own designs. The far future is ours ; the spirits of just men made perfect, the great and ever increasing cloud of witnesses, watch our warfare. For us it is a very small thing that we should be judged of man's " day." Our day—our unit of time—is God's day, which, for all we know, may be a thousand years, or a hundred thousand. Let us then go forward with our work, be it here or elsewhere, whithersoever we may be bidden to go. " Show thy servants thy work, and their children thy glory." So the Divine answer to the question, " Are there few that be saved ? " is the simple command, " Strive ye to enter in by the narrow door."

CHAPTER IV

AN UNPOPULAR TEXT

IT is not my intention to discuss St. Paul's beliefs about the resurrection—a very difficult subject. It is plain however from the fifteenth chapter of first Corinthians that he did not believe in a resurrection of the flesh. On the other hand he did not believe that the soul, after it leaves the body, will be "naked." A clothing is prepared for it, a "spiritual body"—a conception which perhaps was not much clearer to himself than it is to us. What moved him most was the thought that Death, almost personified as a malign power and an instrument of the Evil one, has been conquered, robbed of its sting, virtually destroyed, by the resurrection of Christ.

My subject is rather different. Can you think of any other text in the New Testament that is more thoroughly unpopular to-day than "If in this life only we have hope in Christ, we are of all men most miserable"? Anyone who is at all sensitive to the feelings of his audience must have felt, especially if they are working men, that this is emphatically what a modern congregation does *not* want to hear about. Not only is it no part of their religion ; they resent having it put before them. And many of the religious teachers who are most in touch, as the phrase is, with current thought, seem to have no wish to speak on a subject which even to themselves is unwelcome.

This is to me one of the greatest changes that the teaching of Christianity has ever undergone, and it has come about, rather rapidly, between the middle and the end of the last century. The doctrine that we are here on our probation for another life has always, until within living memory, been the cornerstone of Christian ethics. It inspires the grandest medieval hymns, such as the "Dies Irae", and "O Sion Unica", of Bernard of Cluny. The whole civilisation of the Middle Ages, on the spiritual side, is built upon the belief in the two worlds, the present world and the world to come. Nor did the Reformation make any difference. The same splendid promises, the same awful threats, the same exhortations not to set our hearts on the fleeting shadows of time and the good things of the world, resounded from Roman Catholic, Lutheran, Calvinist and Anglican pulpits. The terrors of hell were certainly not left undescribed by Catholics, Presbyterians, Wesleyans or Baptists. Now, in the last seventy-five years, the tradition of eighteen centuries has been broken. Christianity has to all appearance been secularised as it has never been secularised before. It is surely worth while to enquire how this change has come about; for whether we welcome it or not it is an almost revolutionary change. Christianity is becoming a this-worldly religion. This is perhaps what most of us like; and yet there has never been a time, till our own, when Christianity has been so preached. What are the causes of the change? I believe there are several, which have all operated at the same time, thus making the decay of the old tradition more rapid.

First, we are now fully alive to the amazing crudity of the old pictures of bliss and torment. The only wonder is that they were tolerated so long. Near the beginning of the Old Testament, Abraham asks, " Shall not the Judge of all the earth do right? " and has no doubt of the answer. All through the Old Testament, the problem of Divine justice agitates the minds of the Jewish people. God is just; and yet the world as we know it is full of injustice. One explanation after another was tried. The sins of the fathers are visited on the children. The nation and not the individual is the unit. The sufferer is a secret sinner. The good man suffers for a time, and the wicked flourishes like a green bay-tree. But though the troubles of the righteous are great, the Lord delivereth him out of all, while the wicked is rooted out, and his place can nowhere be found. None of these explanations could be made to square with the facts, and at last the sublime idea of the suffering servant, sacrificing himself for the people, arises. Later still in their history, the Jews began to look for compensation beyond the grave. And yet, what are the worst temporal miscarriages of justice compared with the terrible picture of all men and women divided into two classes, one class to be rewarded with endless bliss, the other condemned to endless torment ? Have we ever met or heard of a human being who deserved to be tortured for ever ? It is not so much the duration of the punishment as its character which shocks us. There are many persons whom we cannot imagine living in the presence of God and His saints ; they have excluded themselves from all that we suppose to be the life of heaven. But that the Father of our Lord Jesus Christ is an implacable torturer—that is a strange belief to have lasted for eighteen centuries. No doubt the pictures were painted in glaring colours just because the doctrine was not strongly believed, as the criminal law sometimes threatens with atrocious penalties crimes which are hard to detect. No doubt also disproportionate rewards and punishments were associated with the idea of absolute power ; the monstrous severity of our criminal code excited but little indignation till the nineteenth century. The doctrine of Purgatory was a partial answer to the objection that almost everybody is " over-bad for blessing and over-good for banning." But when all is said, it remains almost incomprehensible to us how sermons

like those of Jonathan Edwards, which contain flowers of
speech like " You cannot stand before an infuriated tiger ;
what then will you do when God rushes upon you in His
wrath ? " were ever preached and eagerly listened to. Such
doctrines, even when they are only half believed, distort the
whole perspective of religion. They engender cruelty ; they
justify persecution ; they encourage immoral beliefs about
absolution and death-bed repentance, or the arrogant confidence and abject despair which arise from the belief in pre-
destination. The Christian doctrine of eternal life had been
so vulgarised, travestied, and divorced from all that we mean
by justice, that nearly all Christians would now sympathise
with the famous outburst of John Stuart Mill, " I will call no
being just who is not what I mean by just when I apply the
word to my fellow-creatures, and if there is a Being who can
send me to his hell for not so calling him, to hell I will go."

But there are other reasons why the other-worldly side of
Christianity has fallen into disfavour. What do we mean by
the other world ? Is it a world which will begin to exist when
this world exists no longer, or is it a world which exists already
in some other part of space ? Our traditional ideas of the
other world are derived partly from space and partly from
time, and the two pictures do not agree very well together.
Both have been made very difficult by the knowledge of the
universe which came to us not in very recent times but as
long ago as Copernicus and Galileo. Until the Renaissance,
there was a theological map of the universe, like a building in
three storeys, with the earth in the centre, heaven above, and
hell beneath. It is not to be supposed that all scholars and
philosophers accepted this literally. It was always orthodox
to say that God has His centre everywhere and His circumfer-
ence nowhere. But there is no doubt that Christians generally
believed that heaven and hell are geographical expressions.

Our Reformers argued against transubstantiation that the natural body of Christ is in heaven, and that it is contrary to the properties of a natural body to be in two places at once. The same is asserted in the Article of Religion about the resurrection and ascension of Christ.

It is one of the strangest things in the history of religion that the bearing of the new knowledge upon dogmatic theology was so slow to be realised. There are many still who do not see how completely it shattered the theological map of the universe. We cannot seriously suppose that any of the millions of stars with which the boundless expanse of space is sparsely sown, has been chosen as the abode of the Creator and of beatified spirits. And if we think of the alternatives which alone are open to us, we cannot picture the risen body of Christ as occupying any position in space. Nor, if we transfer our thoughts to the form of time, do we get any more encouragement from astronomy, if we wish to keep the simple beliefs which we learned in the nursery. I have no wish to enlarge on what to many are painful thoughts. But we must not play tricks with our souls. The scientific view of the universe—even if we allow for certain disturbing factors introduced by Einstein's calculations, is, in its broad outlines, as certainly true as anything in human knowledge, and it leaves no room for a local or temporal heaven. We are living now in an atmosphere of science, whether we are ourselves students of physics or not ; and the imaginative pictures which satisfied our forefathers, even long after the geocentric hypothesis had been abandoned by all educated people, can satisfy us no longer. I cannot doubt that this tremendous change, which has torn our beliefs about the other world out of their setting in space and time, has had a great effect in the secularising of religion of which I spoke. Nor is there, so far as we can see, the slightest prospect that the pictures which we have lost will ever be restored to us. Except as a conscious parable we cannot any longer think of heaven and hell as places, and we ought not to be compelled to assert our belief in doctrines which have no meaning except on the geocentric hypothesis.

There is a third cause of the secularisation of Christianity, quite different from those which have been mentioned. Millenarianism has been a pertinacious superstition, reviving again and again in Church history, at periods of social unrest. The essence of it is the belief that a perfect society will one day be set up on earth. So far as it is held exclusively, it is a kind of substitute for the Christian doctrine of immortality. The Kingdom of God is brought down from heaven to earth, and the time is usually assigned to the near future.

Historians in the future will perhaps say that Millenarianism in a peculiar form took root among progressive thinkers in France in the eighteenth century, that it inspired the French Revolution, and then spread over the civilised world, forming indeed the lay religion of the nineteenth century. It began with the assertion of the perfectibility of man, and was embodied in a supposed law of nature, that evolution means the gradual progress of the universe in general towards a perfect state. Progress, it was assumed, was a universal law, working automatically. It would be difficult to overestimate the effect of this belief, held for the most part with unquestioning confidence, on the politics, science, philosophy, and social life of the nineteenth century. Even to this day anyone who suggests that the world will probably go on in the old ruts for an indefinite period is branded as an extreme pessimist, though the speaker probably finds the world as it is a pleasant enough place to live in. I will not discuss whether this new apocalyptism has stimulated Western Europe and North America to greater exertions. Hope, no doubt, makes people more industrious and efficient. I only point out that though it was enthusiastically endorsed by many men of science in the Victorian Age, it has nothing scientific about it, but is, in fact, a pure superstition, contradicted by science, by history, and by philosophy, and certainly not supported by Christianity. So long as these apocalyptic dreams held the field there was no room for the Christian doctrine of immortality. It was thrust out by a will-of-the-wisp—the idea of a Utopia, gradually but not too slowly to be established here on earth. The extreme apocalyptists, the revolutionary party, regard the doctrine of immortality with anger and contempt. They understand that it banishes their Utopia to a sphere where they at least have no wish to look for it.

We have then three potent causes in the remarkable change of which I have spoken, the transformation of Christianity into a religion of increasing happiness here and now, with no eternal background. The three causes, as I have said, are : the abandonment of the crude and morally shocking pictures of Divine retribution which strangely enough satisfied our ancestors ; the astronomical discoveries which destroyed the traditional Christian cosmography ; and the dream of in- definite and almost automatic progress which filled men's minds from the beginning of the French Revolution to the outbreak of the Great War. It is significant that neither the moral revolt nor the scientific revelation had much effect on popular religious teaching till a rival religion—the idea of pro- gress—began to spread, and to twist the doctrine of evolution to support it. The cynical saying, that a successful religion is a superstition that has enslaved a philosophy, applies accu- rately enough to the religion of human perfectibility. It is Darwin anticipated in caricature by Rousseau.

Many keen observers who have considered this acute secularising of Christianity, are of the opinion that it is the beginning of the end of the great religion which has inspired the civilised world for nearly two thousand years. Before long, they think, nothing will be left of the grand picture of reality which the Church has spread before the eyes of the nations. The Churches, as political or social institutions, may go on for a time ; but the tree is hollow and dead ; it can put forth no more leaves.

I am very far from agreeing with this prediction. Of the three causes which I have mentioned, the first, the purification of our ideas of divine justice is, I think, a pure gain to religion. The third, the will-of-the-wisp, is I think flickering out, though it may lead to one or two more abortive attempts to realise the millennium by revolution. The second is, I admit, a tremendously serious problem. But though it must entail great changes in some ancient and venerated dogmas, I believe it can and will be solved, if the Church will face it with courage and intellectual honesty, and that the outcome will be a gain to spiritual religion.

Let us go back to St. Paul and his unpopular text, "If in this life only we have hope in Christ, we are of all men most miserable." What did he mean by it ? St. Paul was not a man who ran away from earthly life and its problems. He was as great a conqueror as Alexander, in the reverse direction. Alexander carried the Greek language and culture to the borders of India ; St. Paul, if he went to Spain as he intended to do, carried the Gospel of Galilee to the borders of the Atlantic. It was a stupendous undertaking, but he saw that it could be done, and he did it.

His personal religion, as is plain from his epistles, was a Christ-mysticism. The glorified Christ—the Pneuma-Christos —had revealed Himself to St. Paul, and was the guide and inspirer of his life. Therefore for him, Christ had not gone away ; He was present, but as a spiritual power. All that St. John says about Life or Eternal Life, as a present possession, a state to which we have access, though imperfectly, here and now, a kingdom of ultimate and indestructible values in which the soul loses and finds itself, is a legitimate development of the thought of St. Paul. The fourth Gospel is the best commentary on St. Paul's Epistles. Most certainly he looked forward to higher and more blessed experiences after his mortal life was over. "I have a desire to depart and to be with Christ, which is far better." But I think it would not be going too far to say that the greatest change for him was not the change from life on earth to life in heaven with Christ, but the change in this present life, which he calls the new birth. That is the death, and the rising again, that supremely matters. After that decisive change, eternal life for us has already begun. Let us think how great an alteration in our ideas about immortality that means. "We know that we have passed from death unto life, because we love the brethren."

St. Paul has his own doctrine of progress. "Now we see through a glass, darkly, but then face to face ; now I know in part, but then shall I know even as also I am known." Our progress is advance in knowledge of the eternally real and true, that internal progress which Clement of Alexandria traces as a journey in three stages from unbelief to faith, from faith to knowledge, from knowledge to love.

I think we may put away the common objection that Christian holiness is too self-centred, a form of selfishness. The plain fact is that the rewards of Christ's service, if they are misunderstood, are not credible to a selfish man ; and if they are understood, they are not attractive to a selfish man. A cool head and a cold heart never yet brought a man to the foot of the Cross. Those who chatter about "individualism" generally want, as Carlyle shrewdly says, "a Gospel of Brotherhood not according to any of the four old Evangelists, calling on men to repent and amend each his own wicked existence, that they might be saved, but a Gospel rather according to a new fifth evangelist, Jean Jacques, calling on men to amend each the whole world's wicked existence, and be saved by making the constitution—a different thing, and distant *toto caelo*."

I believe then that we shall come nearest to St. Paul's conception of immortality if we try to think of eternal life as a kingdom of ultimate values, not mere ideals, but spiritual realities, a world not in space or time, but known to us in part while we live here, since Christ came and " brought life and immortality to light." To have hope in Christ in this life only is to be blind to all this, to think of Christ only as a human being who lived a short life in Palestine and preached in the reign of Tiberius, and of His teaching as a promise of " a good time coming." It is true that St. Paul is arguing for the resurrection, a fact in time ; but we must remember that for him the life and death and resurrection of Christ are a great sacrament, a mystery, as the Greeks called it, a type and pattern of the normal spiritual journey of the soul, a path to be trodden by us all. " Even if we once knew Christ after the flesh," he says, " we now know Him so no more." How else can we say that Christ's victory over death is also our victory? For there is no resurrection on the third day for us. " If Christ be not raised, *ye are yet in your sins*." Does not this verse throw a light on his real argument ?

" The Christian religion," says Harnack, " is a sublime and simple thing ; it means one thing and one thing only ; eternal life in the midst of time, by the strength and under the eyes of God." This is finely said, but it is rather the faith of Aristotle than of Christianity, for it does not assert eternal life after this life is ended, and though I am well aware of the contradiction of calling eternity timeless existence, and then introducing the words " before" and "after", I am not content with any statement which seems to leave us no future. " *Quod Deo non perit, sibi non perit,*" says Augustine ; a profound and surely a perfectly valid argument for immortality. Nothing that has value in God's sight can be as if it had never been.

I do not think the astronomical knowledge already referred to need make us very severe with ourselves in trying to realise the fact of immortality, if only we remember that we are trying to imagine what eye hath not seen, nor ear heard, neither hath it entered into the heart of man to conceive. We believe in an eternal world, where all that is precious in the sight of God is preserved safe for evermore. We believe that love is stronger than death, and that in that life spirits are separated from each other, if they are separated, not by space or time, but only by difference of nature. And we have only our poor human language in which to express these truths and make them real to ourselves. If we try to philosophise, and instead of time and place speak of appearance and reality, or of shadow and substance, we are not really escaping from the categories which we have condemned as inadequate. In talking to simple folk, I never try to deprive them of the pictorial images in which they find comfort : it is enough to give a caution that the reality is no doubt very different from anything that we can imagine. But more often, I think, our task is to show to troubled minds that the deepest truths of our religion are not bound up with these materialistic representations. A spiritual presentation of the Gospel is not an explaining away of what to our hearers are literal facts ; we hope it may be a restoration of the faith which the insecurity of the literal facts threatened to sweep away.

To sum up. Secularism is a sorry substitute for the Christian hope, and its promises are delusive. But the theodicy which it displaced was materialistic, unethical, and incredible, and we are well rid of it. We need not hunt about for a truer conception of eternal life, for it is to be found between the covers of the New Testament, expressed in symbols, as all eschatology must be symbolic, but lofty and spiritual. " We look not at the things which are seen, but at the things which are not seen. For the things which are seen are temporal, but the things which are not seen are eternal."

CHAPTER V

AN UNCHARTED JOURNEY

TO the younger men and women of to-day, I desire, with God's help, to offer some little guidance on the larger problems of life now opening before them. To interpret the signs of the times is a task which no one should attempt without great humility and diffidence. I cannot expect, or even wish, that all should agree with me. I can only offer you the best that I have to give on some of the questions which are exercising the minds of all thoughtful men.

It is probable that some are almost bewildered by the absolute freedom of thought and discussion which marks society to-day. Traditional beliefs and habits, hitherto treated with respect, are questioned or even ridiculed. Religious observances are neglected; revolutionary opinions on politics, sociology, art, and even morals, are confidently advocated; everything seems to be in the melting-pot, even the dogmas of nineteenth-century science, even the discoveries connected with the mighty names of Newton and Darwin. It is not a time when a senior man, whatever his official position, can deal magisterially with these difficulties, as if they were perplexing only to immature minds. The facts are far otherwise. A clever caricaturist has represented the modern man contemplating a gigantic note of interrogation. That is really the attitude of the post-war world. The dogmatist is, for the time being, silenced. We are all alike uncertain as to what the morrow will bring forth, in science, in politics, in philosophy, and in religion. "We see not our tokens: there is not one prophet more "—or perhaps we have too many minor prophets.

And yet it is not, as has been unwisely said, " a new world since the war." It is the old world, and the old battle between the worse and the better, the better and the best. Even the problems are mainly the same ; only the course of events has been speeded up in some ways by a great convulsion, and retarded in other ways. The normal evolution of ideas and ideals has been disturbed. The war broke some of the threads which secured continuity with the past ; these must be joined again. Let us recall the words of Mazzini, one of the liberators of Italy. " Those only should utter the sacred name of Progress whose souls possess intelligence enough to comprehend the past, and whose hearts possess sufficient poetic religion to reverence its greatness. The temple of the true believer is not the chapel of a sect ; it is a vast Pantheon." It is our duty to stimulate this intelligence and to excite this reverence. Contempt for their parents' opinions is a besetting sin of the young ; you may be sure that thirty years hence your children will be equally disdainful of yours. Our business is to be always learning and never forgetting ; to preserve traditions without undue subservience to them.

We must of course be willing to consider great problems from the Christian point of view, and I wish to deal briefly with three of them, as they are likely to meet us in conversation or in our reading. The three problems are : the social question, marriage and the family, and Christian belief.

As Christians we are not, I think, bound to attach ourselves to one political party rather than another. Historically, it is quite untrue that Christ came to preach an economic revolution. The Gospel is a message of spiritual redemption, not of social reform. Some of the Old Testament prophets plunged into the turbid waters of political agitation ; Christ walked over them dryshod. He did not even discourage the apocalyptic dreams which meant so much to His disciples, and which almost destroyed their interest in the future of society. It is as vain to look in the Gospels for political guidance as it is to look in them for any idea of an institutional Church. We should perhaps have been glad to find such help in the Gospels, but it is not there. The plain truth is that our Lord was quite indifferent to all forms of government, ecclesiastical and civil; that He disclaimed any concern with questions of distribution; and that He despised all the paraphernalia of civilisation, beyond the very simplest comforts and necessaries.

I strongly deprecate the violent language often used about our industrial civilisation, which with all its faults is so far the highest achievement of co-operative effort on a large scale. It is not true to say, with an American writer, that " there are no honest goods to buy or to sell," and that " the hideous competitive war makes the industrial order seem like the triumph of hell and madness upon earth." Still less is it true to say with the same writer that " revolution is the Christian's business." Such exaggerated language is foolish, unjust, and mischievous. The large majority of business men live not by robbing their fellows, but by serving them. As Bishop Westcott said, " the honourable purchaser and the honourable seller meet in business for the work of citizens. Their interest is the same—the right support of life." " The permanent stability and efficiency of business depend not on the evils which disfigure it but on the virtues which it promotes. . . . If it were not the general practice of business men to tell the truth and keep their contracts, the fabric of modern trade, which rests on credit, would crumble in a night." [Peabody] The system indeed requires, and has created, a higher average level of integrity and honest service than any other that the world has seen. Vague declamations about the intolerable conditions of modern industry do no good whatever, and a vast amount of harm.

The best way, I think, of looking at our class struggles is that they are a scramble for the enormous unearned increment created, not by capital, nor by labour, but by the new machinery. It cannot be said to belong to anybody, and that is why it is fought for, as two hives of bees will massacre each other for a lump of honey lying between them. The amount of this unearned wealth would be colossal if the possessors of it had not squandered most of it in fighting, a kind of folly which the Church has hitherto failed to stop. The workers also have sometimes diminished the national wealth by disloyal and unwise conspiracies.

Much is being done towards the humanisation of industry, and with this Christians must be in sympathy. But I do not think that as Christians we ought to mix in the bitter quarrels about mere distribution. These quarrels are waged on both sides in a spirit of sheer acquisitiveness; the fight, as Sir Cecil Spring Rice says in one of his letters, " is of selfishness against selfishness, everyone is anxious to gain at the expense of someone else." The Church will only smirch itself by taking part in it.

Am I arguing that Jesus Christ has nothing to say to us as employers or employed ? Far from it. He had a social ideal. Whosoever will be chief among you, let him be your servant, even as the Son of Man came not to be ministered unto, but to minister. The Law of Service is the Christian Law ; and it is a law which our generation is increasingly willing to accept. I know the word " Service " may become unreal or wearisome ; but it embodies the true message of Christ to the business world. Everyone of us has to find out what God meant him to do with his life—in what way he may employ his five talents, or two, or one talent, best ; and then he ought to choose that career, without thinking too much whether it is lucrative or not, and to put his best work into it, without thinking too much whether he is getting a full return for whatever he puts in. Most earnestly I beg you to bear this in mind in choosing a profession. The right work for you is the work which you can do best, work which you can enjoy doing for its own sake ; and this is the main secret of happiness in life ; for in middle life your work will be your play, and your play merely recreation.

I am also convinced that though the Gospel refuses to give us any rulings about distribution, it has a great deal to teach us about consumption, and that the importance of right spending has been much underestimated by social reformers. If we thought more frequently what our money is worth in terms of human labour—if we remembered that to waste ten shillings is to waste, to render nugatory, a whole honest day's work by somebody or other, a great deal of vulgar and selfish expenditure would be stopped.

For remember ; that which in your best moments you desire for yourselves—that your work shall be something which you feel to be worth doing, something which as a man you can be proud of doing well—must also be your ideal for those who directly or indirectly work for you. We have no right to waste the honest work of anybody, and no right to set anybody to do for us work which it is degrading to a free man to have to do. This principle will carry us a long way ; and when I read statistics of the way in which boundless wealth is wasted and destroyed in the richest country in the world, I am inclined to think that right consumption is more important even than right distribution. It is the consumer, not the capitalist, who is to blame if a large part of the labour which the workers have to do is justly felt by them to be degrading.

Every man has a right to be making or doing something which he knows to be useful or believes to be beautiful. Every citizen has a right to " do his bit " for his country in peace as in war, and most men, in every class of life, would like to do it if they were allowed.

These are fragmentary remarks on a great subject, but I think they are true as far as they go.

I pass to the second group of problems, those connected with marriage and the family. Periods of Puritanism and of licence seem to alternate ; we are now in a period of licence, in which the principles which have held society together since a time earlier than the dawn of history are too often set aside as irrational taboos. And yet no nation has ever prospered in which family life was not held sacred. Our imaginative literature is now deeply corrupted. There is nothing for which Englishmen have more reason to thank God than for the purity and wholesomeness of English fiction, from Sir Walter Scott to Anthony Trollope. It is true that the romantic movement exaggerated the part which sex plays in a normal human life ; but it was a sublimated eroticism, purified and idealised. Now, in the new books which are being read to-day, the element of sex is much more exaggerated and degraded to rank sensuality. This is not high art, it is not a true picture of human life ; it is just commercialised literature, a prostitution of the intellect. Listen to the instructions given by an American editor to his authors. " Here's a man, see ? And his wife, see ? And another man. Write about that. And let the shadow of the bed be on every page, but never let the bed appear." It seems that there are millions who enjoy these scabrous stories of a foul vice, and I cannot doubt that they are responsible for the break-up of many homes. But I repeat that they are not a true picture of human life. The large majority of marriages are faithful and happy. A happy marriage is the best thing in human life, and it will be within the reach of almost all of you. God is love ; and the love of husband and wife brings us nearer to the heart of reality, the knowledge of God, than any other experience. The profanation of a sacrament is a very ugly thing, and I cannot understand why anyone should find the subject attractive.

Our Lord's teaching on the subject is plain so far as this —that He regarded marriage as a holy thing, which in the intention of God is indissoluble. He was not a legislator ; and I am not prepared to say dogmatically that He would never have sanctioned release from the marriage-vow in very hard cases. Hard cases, it has been said, make bad law ; but it is a bad law which multiplies hard cases. It is conceivable that He who said, " The Sabbath was made for man, not man for Sabbath," might have said, if He had been confronted with a very hard case, " Marriage was made for man, not man for marriage." But when He spoke on the subject, He was not thinking of the occasional wreckage of a marriage, but of its normal conditions—of what it was meant to be, ought to be, and in most cases actually is. Adultery may be the pastime of the idle rich ; the very idea of it ought no more to occur to your minds than the idea of forging a cheque.

I come to the third and last of my three topics—the position of the Christian religion in the world of to-day, its message to the present generation, and its prospects for the future. And here it is probable that I must ask some to bear with me if I find difficulties and problems where they see none. If it is our business as Christians and Churchmen, not to " prove all things ", but only to " hold fast that which is good "; if we are not runners carrying a lighted torch, but only custodians of a deposit ; if we have not to seek for a truth which is already in our possession ; if the faith once delivered to the saints suffices us, even though it be encumbered by primitive science and obsolete philosophy; if the authority of the Church precludes all inquiry into questions which an infallible tradition has decided once for all; then our task is certainly simplified, and we shall have only to pronounce upon much of modern thought a verdict of unqualified condemnation. I shall not wittingly give offence to those who think it enough *stare super antiquas vias ;* but I cannot take this position myself. My view on the present and future of Christianity is not unlike that of Rudolf Eucken, whose conclusion, in his book called *Can we still be Christians ?* is, " We not only can but must be Christians; only however on the one condition that Christianity be recognised as a progressive historical movement, still in the making." But still more I owe my indebtedness to Ernst Troeltsch, whom Baron Von Hügel, in spite of the difference in their creeds, regarded as the deepest theological thinker in our generation. I agree with him that a Church-directed civilisation, a religion and ethics based on external authority, is no longer possible. Authority is the method of the teacher of immature pupils; but the time comes when the pupils grow up, and then the good teacher tries to make himself superfluous; he welcomes the growing independence of his pupil's mind; he wishes him to think for himself and be guided by the judgment which his teacher has helped to form. Christianity, it may be, has reached the adult, no longer the adolescent stage. The transition from authority to experience is in progress; the spiritual life, as Eucken is not tired of saying, is and must be autonomous, bearing with it its own credentials and its own progressive verification.

In holding this view of revelation as a progressive spiritual enlightenment we are not false to the history of Christianity. We look back to those very bold pioneers, St. Paul and the author of the Fourth Gospel, who surely, as compared with the Palestinian Church, were the progressives of their day.

We think of Clement of Alexandria and his picture of the Christian " Gnostic "—he is not yet afraid of the word ; of the fruitful labours of the other Greek Fathers to interpret Christianity in the terms of the philosophy of their time ; of the Aristotelianism and Platonism of St. Thomas Aquinas and the other great schoolmen ; of the great German idealists and the independent work of British philosophers on the same lines.

We shall be false to the spirit of these pioneers if we take their results as final ; it is their method, their confident faith, their intellectual honesty, their forward view, which we should take as our models.

It is one of the great services of Troeltsch to historical philosophy that he has shown how little modern Protestantism, at least in educated circles, has to do with the doctrines of Luther and Calvin, though at the same time he finds that in the Reformed Churches there is far more chance for Christianity to enter into a fruitful alliance with the best secular culture, than in the countries which have remained faithful to the Roman obedience. Luther and Calvin both belong to the Middle Ages, which in truth they helped to prolong. They, like their Roman opponents, wished for a religion of authority ; they were not tolerant ; they were not friends of freedom. Even the peculiar secular asceticism of Calvin, which brought into existence that curious product, the modern business man, has almost disappeared, though it lingers in America and Scotland. The progressive forces in religion to-day come partly from the Renaissance tradition, partly from mystical experience, the religion of the inner light, and partly from the individualism, liberty and zeal for social reform which characterised the sectaries, those step-children of the Reformation, who obtained a short and troubled supremacy under Oliver Cromwell, and whose ideas are now very much in the ascendant.

These three forces all point to an autonomous and progressive religion, quite different from Catholicism and the earlier Protestantism. There is not the slightest tendency, among those who think as I do, to question the divine authority of Jesus Christ, or to build on any other foundation than that which was laid in the Gospels and Epistles. Nor is there anything really new in the idea of a Church of the Spirit, which beckons us on by untried paths. It is an attempt to gather together and twine into one threefold cord, not to be quickly broken, three of the threads which can easily be traced throughout Church History.

First, there is the friendly understanding with Humanism and Science, which was broken off by the disastrous wars of religion, and has never been cemented again. Here the Church has a great leeway to make up. I do not mean that we should go to Science for our philosophy; in that field we have much more to teach than to learn; nor that we should be in a hurry to fit into our frame of theology mathematical, physical, and biological theories which may be superseded before we have succeeded in understanding them. But I am sure we ought to recognise that the life of the Spirit is one, and that God is now revealing Himself by means of the astonishing discoveries which are being made every year in the natural order. The Church of the future must make friends with her quondam allies and sometime enemies, Humanism and Science. God knows we need all the allies we can get against secularism, against materialism, against the rising tide of sensuality. It is not as if scientific men were still dogmatic materialists or dogmatic agnostics. I cannot forget the help and sympathy we received from leading men in the scientific world at a recent Conference of Modern Churchmen. We Churchmen have much to learn from the scientific temper, pure, dry, and bracing, like mountain air. But that you may not think that I am suggesting a complete surrender, consider this, which I have not heard said before, and which I think is worth saying. The nature of God is admittedly reflected very imperfectly in the human mind. Why should we think that it is mirrored more completely in external nature? The throne of the Godhead, as was said fifteen hundred years ago, is the mind or spirit of man.

The Church of the Spirit must make friends with Humanism and Science. For the primary ground of its faith, it must rest on the second of my "three threads", on what it is the fashion to call religious experience, but which our forefathers called the testimony of the Holy Spirit. This means not only the life of prayer, though emphatically it does mean that; it means also that we must respect the conscience of our age when it acquits or condemns us for actions which ecclesiastical tradition perhaps judged rather differently. There are real changes in Christian ethics; I must not give instances, since I have not time to give reasons here. But we must not let it be said that the Church is reactionary in these matters; the peril is not imaginary. The Church is really in danger when its teaching causes a moral revolt in candid minds.

Lastly, we may learn from the despised sectaries of the seventeenth century, not only the duty of toleration, which we have assimilated already, but to throw aside all claims to a monopoly of grace for any institutional organisation; claims which have a disastrously great survival-value for the corporation which asserts them, but which may easily make that corporation a curse rather than a blessing to humanity. As for the zeal of these sectaries to set up a Kingdom of God, or a reign of the saints, on earth, I have already said something. Christianity is a revolutionary idealism, which estranges revolutionists because it is idealistic, and conservatives because it is revolutionary. Its treatment of current values is revolutionary; its attitude to established institutions is not revolutionary, because it knows that no political alchemy will produce golden conduct out of leaden instincts. Hence arise many moral problems and questions of conscience. But always remember this. The method of Christ is from within outwards, from the heart of man to the social order. We must choose between the methods of Christ and those of Rousseau or Marx.

These then are my hopes, my dreams if you will, for the Church of the future. They may be all wrong, or they may be all right, yet not destined to be fulfilled. For all I know, though I do not think so, we may be heading towards another Dark Age.

We cannot however remind ourselves too often, when we say "we walk by faith not by sight", that stress should be laid on the verb. Faith is a way of walking, not a way of talking, or as Benjamin Whichcote put it, Christianity is a divine life, not a divine science. If we only talk, we shall very likely come to the conclusion that Christianity is played out. If we try to live in such a way that Christ would approve our life, we shall certainly not think that. "Lord, to whom should we go? Thou hast the words of eternal life." There are some permanent acquisitions of the human spirit, from which it cannot go back, and of these the Christian revelation is the greatest. It is a principle of life, and it can therefore change, as only the permanent can change. But to us, as to past ages, it can be and will be the guiding light which we may follow over the uncharted country through which our path lies. It has not failed us who are old; it will not fail you who are young. But unless you follow the gleam, you will soon see it no longer. Faith begins as an act of will, " the resolution to stand or fall by the noblest hypothesis." " Who chooseth me must give and hazard all he hath." Explain it how we will, that is the condition of spiritual vision. It makes the popular talk about the decay of Christianity sound very trivial.

It was a saying of Renan, which proves the fundamental frivolity of his outlook upon life, that in order to understand a religion one ought to have believed, and then to have ceased to believe in it. Far truer are the words of Otto : " He who professes to stand outside religion, and to view all the religions of the world in impartial detachment, will never understand any of them." You will find some of these superior persons in every learned society—honorary members of all religions ; and they will have very little to teach you. Christianity can only be understood from inside ; and those who are inside know Him in whom they have believed. " I am persuaded," says St. Paul, " that neither death nor life, nor height nor depth, nor any other creature, can separate us from the love of God which is through Christ Jesus our Lord."

CHAPTER VI

THE DEDICATED LIFE

WHEN our Lord says "For their sakes I consecrate myself," He admits us to the sanctuary of His human will, when He is preparing Himself for the supreme act of sacrifice. He consecrates Himself for His disciples, and He consecrates them for His service and for their brethren. Christians in 1 Corinthians are "the consecrated in Christ Jesus"; the writer to the Hebrews uses the word several times. Let us consider what this should mean for ourselves.

We will not use the word "consecration", which sounds a little too exalted for us. We will speak, instead, of the *dedicated* life. Dedication implies that a man should have a clear idea of what he believes, what he wishes to do with his life, and what he desires his life on earth to be. Or, as Lord Haldane said to the students at Edinburgh University, "the first duty of life is to comprehend clearly what our strength will let us accomplish, and then to do it with all our might."

These are, of course, very old counsels. You are to find out, says the Roman satirist, Persius, what kind of man God has commanded you to be, and what is your place in the life of mankind. Or, as Pindar puts it, "find out what you are, and become it"—make it so, in nautical phrase.

But this is, perhaps, to ask too much of those who have only lately reached man's estate. You do not yet know your own characters, or what you are good for, for your characters are not fully formed, and your capacities are still growing. For this reason, it is often a mistake to press boys at school to

E

make up their minds about their profession or trade, unless the conditions make an early choice necessary, or unless a definite career is clearly marked out for them. In particular, I doubt whether it is wise for a boy to make up his mind to be a clergyman, unless he feels a strong vocation. The ministry is a calling which needs a mature choice; in some cases even twenty-three is too young. Or I should rather say, a boy or youth is right to *think* seriously about it, but in no way to pledge himself.

So when I speak of the dedicated life to young men and women I do not mean that you should all plot out your future careers, as if the question " Lord, what would'st Thou have me to do ? " were easily and quickly answered. Dedication is not to a career, but to a service—the service of God and our fellow-men, whatever your future work may be. And in making this kind of dedication I say that you cannot afford to wait. Characters are generally to a great extent determined for life between the ages of twelve and twenty-five; these are the formative years.

Let me commend to you this saying of Bernard Shaw. " A gentleman is a man who tries, in one form or another, to put into life at least as much as he takes out of it." In all ranks of society, the world is divided into those who lift and those who lean; those who bear their share of the world's burden, and those who are clever enough to trip along unencumbered, leaving others to carry their loads. I know that the social order under which we live (and indeed any other social order) makes it difficult to apply this principle. We no longer define a gentleman as a man who does no work; but we do still think of success as getting more and too often giving less than other people. Of course there are many ways of serving our generation; but whichever way we choose, we are the servants of Him Who said, " He that will be great

among you, let him be your minister " ; and " I am among you
as he that serveth." And if we are able to get positions which
the world thinks rather lucky we should consider that our
responsibilities are increased. Much is required of him to
whom much is given. I am not a Socialist; but Bernard
Shaw's maxim is the Christian equivalent of socialism, the law
of equivalent service. It should be a point of honour to us
that the world shall be somehow a gainer, or at least not a loser,
by our sojourn in it.

This, then, is one part of the dedicated life—the resolve to
pay our way by giving at least as much as we receive. It is
difficult, not only because it is impossible to weigh one kind
of service against another, but because most of our debt is due
to the past, and debts to the past can only be discharged by
putting posterity in our debt, a duty which seems to belong
to those who have five talents, not two or one, like ourselves.
But the principle of not wasting time or money or anything
else, when we might dedicate it to service of some kind, is, I
am sure, one which ought never to be forgotten.

I am not going to suggest to you that the highest form of
dedicated life is the ministry of the Church. We are perhaps
too prone to think that a life concerned with higher things is
necessarily a higher life. The spirit in which we do our work,
whatever it is, is much more important than the subjects which
have to engage our attention. But I do think that the shortage
in candidates for ordination is a regrettable thing, and I do not
altogether understand it. The ministry is no doubt a poorly
paid profession, and intellectual difficulties may count for
something, though I do not think they count for much; for
the bishops, or some of them, at any rate, are very open-
minded; but I believe what deters young men most is the
suspicion that it is not really a noble profession. Men say
they want to do some "real work", or "a man's job", if it is

only some humble drudgery on the lower rungs of the business ladder. That is the false notion which I want to combat— that work for religion is not real work, not a man's job. The great Oxford philosopher, F. H. Bradley, will not be suspected of being a clerical advocate. But this is what he says about religion. " We can see at once that there is nothing more real than what counts in religion. To compare facts such as these with what comes to us in outward existence would be to trifle with the subject. The man who demands a reality more solid than that of the religious consciousness knows not what he says." This great thinker sees that in the religious con- sciousness we have an adumbration of that higher synthesis of experience which is the object of his quest. The relig- ious mind, in so far as it is really religious, is in touch with reality.

Nothing, it seems to me, is more important than that the Church should include among its ministers a large number of men who are really educated and seriously minded, who have thought out things for themselves and understood what the Christian religion really means. Modern philosophy is full of the conception of *Value*. Well, Christianity rests upon a standard of values, which we can easily find in the New Testa- ment. It is, of course, not merely an intellectual theory. But it has its own standard, a very definite standard; and this is why it is so necessary to present it plainly to the world at the present time, when our post-war society seems to have no standards. Our generation believes in adventure and in kindness—in giving others a good time, and in what else ? Not very much, it seems to me. We need something more heroic and more serious than this. We have thrown away the last vestiges of asceticism, and have no heroism to take its place. And this is a peculiarly difficult time, when a survey of the world shows us that liberty is in great danger, just because men have not enough character or wisdom to govern themselves, and are too narrow and selfish to govern others. Has Christianity a moral and social message, by which I do not at all mean a political message? Do we not see that our civilisation is threatened by the chaotic motives which sway the actions of men—by excessive love of pleasure and amusement, by aversion from hard work, and by acquisitiveness, with the bitterness and jealousy which it fosters? I should be the last to deny that there are many good features in our post-war civilisation, notably the really civilising influence of some of the new discoveries, especially broadcasting, which puts the results of science, learning, and art within the reach of everybody, and widens thereby the mental horizon of at least half the population. But the blight of secularism and triviality is over it all; it just lacks the idealism, the aspiration, the heroism which earnest convictions only can inspire. If the ministers of Christ can rise to this conception of their vocation, that it is their office to make real to our people what Bismarck used to call the *imponderables*, the higher values, they need not fear that their work is unpractical.

There is another aspect of the ministerial life which may make it intensely interesting—I mean the scientific and yet sympathetic study of human nature. If the clergy would realise that all their most useful work is done with individuals, and that their main business is to study character—psychology if you will—they would soon be absorbed in what Pope calls the proper study of mankind. If you want to fill a row of narrow-necked vessels with water, you do not dash a bucket over them—which is what I am doing now—you go to each of them separately. I am convinced that this aspect of the clerical life—that the clergy should be physicians of the soul, and sympathetic but acute observers of human nature—will make the work of the clergyman of the future immensely

interesting and useful. We want to take the scientific study
of character out of the hands of the Freudians and psycho-
analysts. The Church has an older and better empirical
tradition of mind-cure, which we Anglicans have neglected
far too much. It is not perfect, by any means, but it is a
sound foundation to build upon. For these reasons I do ask
young men to regard the ministry as one of the possibilities
open before them, and as a very worthy choice, if they feel
that they can put into it all that there is in them.

Men soon divide themselves into two classes—those who
have a definite purpose in life, some clear notion of what they
mean to do and to be, and those who have none. " Let your
loins be girded about and your lamps burning." I wish we
did not see so many young men of very fair abilities, who seem
to be preparing a napkin for their *two* talents.

Of course there are unworthy ambitions, which save a
man from some temptations, but which do not bring a man
peace at the last. I have known successful men, as the world
counts success, of whom it might be said, " He gave them their
desire, and sent leanness withal into their souls." A lean soul
with a professional reputation and a large income is not a good
bargain. " What shall it profit a man ? " said our Lord, who
weighed everything in a scale very unlike that of the world.
I do not deprecate an honourable ambition. ' A little glory
mixed with humbleness cures both a fever and lethargicness."
But the dedicated man has to consider how far he can afford
to play the great game without interfering with his main
purpose, which is to serve God and do good in his generation
with all his heart and mind and soul and strength.

When an elderly man looks back upon his early life, he
wants to help the young to avoid some of the mistakes which
he made himself. My conscience tells me that my own worst
fault as a young man was not slackness but over anxiety about

my future—anxiety not so much to win success as to avoid humiliating failure, of which I was never really in much danger. This may have been partly a matter of temperament ; but I know I should have been much happier if I had made just that act of self-dedication which I am pressing upon you. " Show thou me the way that I should walk in, for I lift up my soul unto Thee. Take me with my faults and capacities, such as they are, and use me as Thou seest fit. Lo, I come to do Thy will, O God." When that choice has been made, a man gains an inward peace and serenity which is reflected in his outward demeanour. He can enjoy the little humours of life and take its ups and downs good-naturedly, because he has come to see things in their true proportions. He is not careful and troubled about many things, because he knows that most things do not matter very much. Thus to dedicate oneself may be as necessary and salutary for those who are naturally disposed to take life too hard as for those who are naturally disposed to take it too easy.

But perhaps in substituting the word " dedicate " for the " consecrate " or " sanctify " of the New Testament, I have missed something which the great high-priestly prayer of Christ was meant to teach us. I think I have missed something, and I must try to pick it up. " For their sakes I consecrate or sanctify myself." The words holiness and saintliness are not popular ; but we must not forget that as Christians we are called to something more than active, cheerful usefulness. At the very heart of Christianity is the belief that the Holy Spirit of God, who is the glorified Christ under another form, dwells within us, " unless we be reprobates." And therefore, as St. Paul says, " I beseech you, by the mercies of God, that ye present your bodies a living sacrifice, holy, acceptable to God, which is your reasonable service." Your reasonable service—λογικὴ λατρεία. Instead of the outward cere-

monies and sacrifices of the Old Covenant, we present ourselves to God, a sacrifice, but a living sacrifice. And as
nothing impure or maimed could be presented to God, we
must see to it that our whole personality—spirit, soul, and
body—is preserved blameless, so far as that is possible. If we
grieve or quench the Spirit, that sanctifying presence will
leave us. " Ye are not your own. Ye are bought with a price.
Therefore glorify God in your body and in your spirit, which
are God's." Dedication to God is a very solemn thing.
" The temple of God is holy, which temple ye are. If any man
defile the temple of God, him shall God destroy."

And this consecration is to be for the sake of others as well
as for ourselves. " For their sakes I consecrate myself." We
are helping or hindering others every day of our lives, not by
what we do or say, but by what we are. There are some men
in whose presence evil is ashamed. We are always the better
for their company. And there are others of whom the opposite
must be said. It is not necessary to show much deliberately,
for concealment is impossible. Our minds are dyed the colour
of our leisure thoughts, and the inner man makes the outer.
Transparency of character is one of the marks of the Christian,
who has nothing to hide. We may think of 1 Corinthians xiii,
which a classical scholar has declared to be the finest thing
written in Greek since the old Athenian masters, and enumer-
ate, with the apostle, all the marks of Love or Charity as they
show themselves in the life and conversation of the true
Christian. Or we may remember that other remarkable
passage where the apostle, contrary to his wont, appeals to
the heathen ideals " virtue " and the desire of " praise."
" Finally, my brethren, whatsoever things are true, whatsoever
things are honourable, whatsoever things are just, whatsoever
things are pure, whatsoever things are lovely, whatsoever
things are of good report, if there be any virtue and if there

be any praise, think on these things." It is as if he said, " For once I appeal to you not as Christians but as gentlemen."

Yes, it is a hard thing that is required of us, or would be if we were judged by what we are and not by what we are trying to be. To begin with, at any rate, all that matters is that we should set our faces in the right direction, and, as St. Peter says in a verse badly translated in the Authorised Version, " Sanctify Christ in your hearts as God." Think of Him at odd moments during the day, and say " Make me a clean heart, O God, and renew a right spirit within me. Cast me not away from Thy presence, and take not Thy Holy Spirit from me. O give me the comfort of Thy help again, and stablish me with Thy free Spirit." I attach great importance to these short ejaculatory prayers. They keep us from forgetting God in our work and in our play. The habit once formed will help us to overcome many temptations.

But for us who are no longer young, what kind of dedication can we offer ? There is, I am afraid, a kind of sclerosis of the conscience which often sets in in middle life. We know our characters, and we fear that it is too late to alter them much. We have taken ourselves, as well as our wives, " for better, for worse." Our habits, we think, will keep us fairly straight, and so we cease to struggle. We form few resolutions, and expect to break those which we do form. It would be too severe to say that we consciously keep an account open with the world, the flesh, and the devil ; but there they are, and if they will behave themselves, there they may stay.

Well, we must go on reminding ourselves that in Christ's service there are no exemptions for persons over fifty, and that if we let ourselves drift we shall not stay where we are ; we shall become harder, less scrupulous, less loving. It is terribly difficult to arrest such a process ; but how many people whom we know have entirely escaped it ! Yet what a blessed influence such men and women exercise, quite unconsciously, upon the young, who can see clearly enough if their elders have so lived as never to grieve or quench the Holy Spirit in their hearts. The words " For their sakes I consecrate myself " have a very special, a very frightening force for men in the teaching profession. They have even more need than the young of very frequent prayer.

Our country has bitter need of the best that all its citizens can give it. For civilisation is plainly shooting the rapids, plunging down with unexampled speed to recovery or disaster, we cannot tell which. Of all the books in the New Testament, the Fourth Gospel has the clearest view of inevitable change and evolution. It has also the strongest faith that the presence of the Paraclete will never forsake us. " I have yet many things to say unto you, but ye cannot bear them now. Howbeit when He, the Spirit of truth, is come, He will guide you into all truth." He has come. " God has sent the Spirit of His Son into our hearts, crying Abba, Father." And what do we, too often, say ? " When I have a convenient season I will call for thee."

CHAPTER VII

IDOLS IN THE HEART

THAT terrible verse, " Every man that setteth up his idols in his heart, I the Lord will answer him according to the multitude of his idols," in which we are warned that judicial blindness is the penalty inflicted by God for idolatry in the heart, or as one might say for false ideas which have become false ideals, may perhaps remind some of us of a famous passage in an English classic. There are four kinds of idols, says Francis Bacon, which betray the human mind. They are idols of the Tribe, or of the Cave, or of the Theatre, or of the Market Place. The idols of the Tribe are founded in human nature itself, the intellect of man being like an uneven mirror which distorts the images thrown upon it. We make our rules, and think that nature conforms to them, because we count the hits and not the misses. Moreover, the will and affections constantly interfere with our intellectual processes. Idols of the Cave draw their nature from the peculiar constitution of each, whether mental or bodily, and from his education and circumstances. For instance, some men are trained to note differences, others resemblances ; some are attracted by antiquity, others novelty. We ought to suspect whatever specially captivates our own mind, if we would keep our judgment sound. Still more troublesome are the idols of the Market Place, which come from the associations of words and names. Words for the most part express only simple distinctions, and are unfit instruments for dealing with abstruse or complex ideas. Hence serious disputations often degenerate into verbal wrangles. Lastly, the idols of the Theatre are notions received by us from without, which, like plots on the stage, are neater and more pleasing than the events of real life.

Such is the famous classification of the obstacles to clear mental vision, drawn by one of the shrewdest observers of human nature. The idols of which Bacon spoke are not primarily objects of worship, but phantoms which float between our eyes and the truth of things, preventing us from seeing them as they are. But these phantoms are terribly apt to become or to generate idols in the other sense—that in which Ezekiel says that men set up their idols in their hearts. False standards, by which men so often fashion their lives, are generally first chosen partly through intellectual and partly through moral error. The idol in the heart need not be a very ignoble image. He may have many estimable qualities which make him worthy of admiration ; but he is none the less a phantom, not the true object of worship for human beings in this world.

In a place where there are large numbers of men of the same age, who have inherited much the same traditions and been brought up in the same way, it is inevitable that some of these idols should be rather prominently displayed. Our great schools, with all their conspicuous merits, set up a standard which in the eyes of nearly all observers from outside is faulty in certain points. The usual criticism is that while manliness, honourable conduct, and kindliness are estimated at their true value, and physical strength and skill at more than their true value, neither brains nor industry are sufficiently respected or admired by the typical public school man. I should be very sorry if the ideal of the English gentleman, our best contribution to ethics, ever fell into discredit. But those who are most anxious to see this old English ideal mended

and not ended should be the first to insist that the athlete and
sportsman is not the perfect man whom we are to revere and
copy. This pattern is in fact an anachronism ; and the maxim
of Charles Kingsley, " Be good, sweet maid, and let who will
be clever," is bad advice to Britannia just now.

There are other and baser phantoms which float before
the mind, desiring to be taken into the heart and there en-
shrined. Such are the "ruling passions", to one or another
of which so many fall a prey, the temptations of the world,
the flesh, and the devil. Nor must we forget the very salutary
warnings given by Bacon as to the mischief done by catchwords, party cries and phrases, in misleading mankind. In
religion and politics, the two subjects in which sane judgment
is most important, the evil is rampant. These catchwords,
for some occult reason, have a wonderful power of producing
mental excitement, and inhibiting any further rational reflection. It is unnecessary to illustrate this from politics, though
one can hardly talk to a vehement young politician without
hearing some meaningless shibboleth uttered in impassioned
tones. In religious questions we see the same readiness to
quote some party slogan, and to inflame the spirit of comba-
tiveness and uncharitableness with the help of it. A great deal
of theological controversy consists in the hurling to and fro
of these verbal missiles, which remind us of the state of things
which St. Paul found at Corinth. " I am of Paul," " I of
Apollos." Sometimes, when the machinery of agitation is
called in to fan the flame, the demoralisation is almost complete, and the idol in the heart has nothing Christian about
it except the name. The idolatry may be a blind loyalty to
authority and tradition as such, without any understanding
of the conditions under which the old customs and beliefs,
once right and natural, are so no longer. " Our Lord called
Himself the Truth ; He never called Himself tradition," says

Tertullian. It is surely a great blunder to make a fetish of tradition, as if a bad custom became respectable by growing old. The Church is very reluctant to acknowledge any moral duties which are not stamped by its own mint. But there are such duties ; and we do not show respect to the bold pioneers who founded the Church by refusing to budge from the position which they occupied. Besides, Christianity was partly paganised and barbarised in becoming the established religion of the Roman Empire. If we still believe in a God who is subject to sudden anger, who likes to be approached with flattery and presents, whose ear can be gained by petitioning those in attendance upon Him, who shows His power, like an Eastern sultan, by the prodigality of his rewards and the ferocity of his punishments, who can change his mind and revoke his purpose, is not such a God an idol ?

It was said long ago by the author of *Ecce Homo*, that the average scientific man worships just at present a more awful and as it were a greater deity than the average Christian. This is only a half-truth ; but when one reads old-fashioned theology, not yet extinct, in which motives and actions are thoughtlessly applied to the Deity which fall far below the best human morality, we can understand Sir John Seeley's protest. As for the attitude of science to religion, and of religion to science, there has been a great improvement in manners on both sides, and a real wish to understand each other. It is not a new phenomenon that astronomers are keenly interested in religion. But we must not suppose that the problems which divide us are solved or nearly solved. This is not so.

There is a very common and very pathetic kind of idolatry among the clergy ; pathetic, because it arises out of an enthusiastic loyalty to old traditions, and the unquestioning obedience of the good soldier. It is not easy to realise that in making the advance of the Church or even the glory of God

the motive of our actions we may be committing idolatry.
But so it is. One of my favourite divines, John Smith, the
seventeenth-century Cambridge Platonist, says wisely: "It is
not the thinking of God's glory that is glorifying of Him.
As all the other parts of religion may be apishly acted over by
fancy and imagination, so may the internal parts be acted over
with much seeming grace by our fancy and passions. Our
Saviour hath best taught us what it is to glorify God—
—namely, to be fruitful in all holiness. We best glorify Him
when we grow most like Him." The history of the great
Society which has taken " ad maiorem Dei gloriam " as its
motto, is the standing instance of how the God of truth,
justice and mercy may be outraged by fanaticism dedicated
to His own service. It is hardly possible to exaggerate the
mischief which idolatry of the Church as a political institution
has done to the cause of Christianity.

Traditions of the elders are part of this idolatry. Men
form an idea of the Bride of Christ, the faith once delivered
to the saints. They idealise and idolise the past history of this
society, which in truth has had a very chequered record, and
then show their loyalty by standing fast, as they say, on the
old paths. Assuredly it is true that other foundation can no
man lay but that which is laid, even Jesus Christ. But in
theological architecture the foundation is too often ingeni-
ously supported by the superstructure, and the superstructure
is not always sound. The failure of much of devoted Church
work is due to the unworthy doctrines about God which we
have inherited as part of the tradition. If we offer to our
people stale gobbets of barbarism instead of the bread of life,
can we wonder if they will not take them ? For it is certain
that no faith which does not appeal to men as something
purer and nobler than the view of life which they might have
without it, can win its way except among the degenerates who

naturally attach themselves to a poor, weak, sensuous cult. There are forms of Christianity, as of other religions, which seem specially adapted to provide an euthanasia for decadent minds ; but the sane and sound will only listen to the very highest moral teaching that has yet been revealed to mankind ; and much of our traditional theology falls far below it. Few things are more pitiable than the sight of wood, hay, stubble, brought with infinite labour and self-sacrifice to God's temple, all because some one of these phantoms of the cave, or the market place, or the theatre, has been set up in the heart and worshipped instead of the true God, who does not reveal Himself to partisans or to bigots, or to those who make the word of God of no effect by their traditions.

What is the meaning of the words, " I, the Lord, will answer him according to the multitude of his idols " ? And of the yet harsher words which follow : " If the prophet be deceived and speaketh a word, I, the Lord, have deceived that prophet " ? We know that as the Proverbs says, " There is a way which seemeth right unto a man, but the end thereof are the ways of death." That is sad enough. But must we admit that there is a dark converse to the saying that God helps those that help themselves ? If God sends us a strong delusion, what hope is there of recovering the truth ? If God be against us, who can be for us ?

The prophet Ezekiel is the strongest upholder in the Old Testament of the equal justice of God to individuals. He stands out as the staunch opponent of fatalism, of foreordained reprobation. God is not the author of evil, neither tempteth He any man. Ezekiel does not impugn the justice of God ; but he throws the guilt back upon the act of idolatry. When the idol is once set up in the heart, the darkening of the judgment is inevitable. If what should be the light within us is darkness, how great is that darkness ! For there is a fatal process of action and reaction between our characters and our ideals. Our ideals—our idols—make our characters, and our characters make our idols. Such as we ourselves are or wish to be, such will God appear to us to be. If the idol in the heart is also a stumbling block of iniquity, the perversion will be grievous. But even when the idol is no monster, but a mistaken ideal, must it not mislead us just where we most need guidance?

How then are we to escape this idolatry of the heart? How are we to prevent the insidious entrance of these phantoms which float always before our eyes? There is only one way. "The mind of man," says the old writer Macarius, "is the throne of the Godhead." And unless the true God is there enthroned where He alone ought to dwell, in the inmost sanctuary of the heart, the vacant seat will be occupied by one of these idols. To worship is natural to man; and the ruling passion, in being inducted to this throne in our hearts, is invested with a kind of spurious universality in which its evil consists. The vanity of human wishes has become proverbial, not so much because the things wished for are not good—for in spite of frequent illusions and disappointments our wishes are often for things both good and attainable—but because in setting our hearts upon them we picture them as being what they are not and can never be. We desire them as containing some satisfying good which they do not contain. And so like the author of Ecclesiastes men have often come to regard all objects of human endeavour as vanity and seeking after wind. St. Augustine, in the best known and most frequently quoted words which he ever wrote, said in prayer to God, "Thou hast made us for thyself, and our hearts are unquiet till they rest in thee." When this rest—and rest means unimpeded activity—is attained—when God is sitting on His throne in our hearts—the good things of this world cease to disappoint

F

us. We can enjoy them because they come to us in their true character. We do not idolise them, but use them (to borrow the simile of a French poet) like a bird who, perching for an instant on a slender twig, feels the branch bend under her, but still sings, knowing that she can fly.

Does St. Augustine's saying sound too vague to be useful ? The heart resting in God—does it need to be made more concrete and particular ? Then let us think of some of the revealed attributes of God—of the grandeur of creation, and the wonders of the infinitely great and the infinitely small, which have been made even more marvellous than before by recent discoveries ; of the mysteries of time and eternity, of unity and multiplicity, of the unchangeable revealed in change. Let us think of the love which, though not everywhere apparent, runs as a vital principle through creation, giving us glimpses of the higher unity in which knowledge and will forget their strife and find their claims satisfied ; that love through whom, as Plato says in the Symposium, all the intercourse of God with man is carried on ; that love which finds its fullest expression in the love with which God so loved the world that He gave His Son ; and of the Cross, which explains so much that would otherwise be dark and unintelligible ; or let us think of the beauty of the divine holiness as displayed in the word and works of Christ and of the best of His servants.

These great thoughts will form the background more often than the foreground of our mental pictures ; but half unconsciously they will give their perspective to all of them. And may I once again invite your special attention to the list of good thoughts which St. Paul gives us in the Epistle to the Philippians.

" Finally, my brethren, whatsoever things are true, noble, just, pure, lovely, and of good report, if there be any virtue and if there be any praise, think of, or rather take account of,

these things." There is no room for idols in a mind so filled—
a mind which in its leisure moments falls back spontaneously
on these fruits of the Spirit. And perhaps the second adjective
in St. Paul's list, a word rather hard to translate, ὅσα σεμνά,
has a special message for us. The word seems to indicate all
that is elevated, reverend, noble, serious, in contrast with all
that is trivial, base, contemptible, frivolous. We are bidden
to take account of, to give their proper place to, all such
things.

Now when a man wastes the precious years of early youth,
is it not most often because he has not taken account of, or
thought about, all the things in life that are σεμνά, grave and
great ? That mixture of frivolousness, commonness of mind
and want of reverence, which is most precisely excluded by
St. Paul's adjective, is much more often the cause of failure
than positive vice. A man has no standard by which he can
judge whether he is letting himself become absorbed by things
which are not worthy of his attention. I need not give examples of these silly interests ; the newspapers, or many of
them, exist to cater for them. There is no excuse here for
self-satisfied commonness of mind. The whole genius of a
university is a call to think on ὅσα σεμνά, on all that is
dignified and beautiful and serious. Those who waste their
time here will never have such a chance again, or if they
do they will not be able to take full advantage of it. The
golden years are over at twenty-five ; character then is formed.

Little children, said St. John, keep yourselves from idols.
It sounds like the voice of an old man speaking to the young.
Get your values right and cherish the best hours of the mind.
The mind is dyed the colour of its thoughts.

And yet sometimes we feel that we are obliged to live
among images, *idola*, while we live here. Now we see through
a glass, darkly—through symbols. Every truth is a shadow

except the last. The outward and visible is not unreal, but it is a sacrament of the inward and spiritual. In being what it is, it symbolises something more than it can ever be, save perhaps in God's sight. And so when we love our relations and friends, it is the Christ in them whom we love. When thou seest thy brother, thou seest thy Lord. When we are loyal to our Church, it is not so much the empirical Church, so disappointing in many ways, as the glorious Church of which the type is laid up in heaven, the Church that has no spot or wrinkle or any such thing, being holy and without blemish. And when we love our country, may we not take to ourselves the noble words of the American, Lowell : " Our true country is that ideal realm which we represent to ourselves under the names of religion, duty, and the like. Our terrestrial organisa-tions are but far-off approaches to so fair a model ; and all they are verily traitors who resist not any attempt to divert them from this their original intendment. Our true country is bounded, on the north and the south, on the east and west, by Justice, and when she oversteps that invisible boundary-line by so much as a hair's breadth, she ceases to be our mother."

It looks as if the line between idealism and idolatry is not very easy to draw. It is not very easy, and these lesser idola-tries are not to be blamed, if the ideals which inspire them are worthy and good. He who loves not his home and country and church which he hath seen, how shall he love God, or humanity at large, whom he hath not seen ? And yet, the things that are seen are temporal ; the things that are not seen are eternal.

CHAPTER VIII

PARABLES

ALMOST all teaching consists in comparing the unknown with the known, the strange with the familiar. We are hardly able to explain what anything is, except by saying it is like something else. Not only is the power of seeing resemblances the great secret of poetic diction, as Aristotle says, but prose is also made up of metaphors, some alive and some dead. Our object in using metaphors, or similes, is not always to explain the less by the more familiar. Often it is to throw new light upon a thing, to make it more vivid and more real, by expressing the idea in another language—in the language perhaps of another sense—as when we speak of the silvery sound of a musical instrument, or the softness of an evening landscape. The description of the operations of nature in terms borrowed from human life—in terms of will and purpose—is almost a necessity, and is not avoided even in scientific treatises. No interpretation of things can be given without the free use of metaphor, symbol, or parable.

Religion furnishes the strongest examples of this rule. Men have allowed their imaginations the fullest scope in their attempts to give definiteness and substance to the formless intuitions of the mystical consciousness. The symbols thus created tend to crystallise as rapidly as linguistic metaphors, and mythology is the result. Even among the Jews, who by prohibiting visible representations of the Deity escaped in large measure this danger from the petrifying of religious symbols, we find a religious poetry as full of imaginative pic-

tures as that of other nations. When we read in the eighteenth
Psalm that Jehovah rode upon the cherubim and did fly, and
came flying upon the wings of the wind ; that he made darkness his secret place, his pavilion round about him with dark
water, and thick clouds to cover him, we have before us word-
pictures which differ only in the medium of representation
from the drawings of William Blake. A curious example of
this universal human tendency is the acted parable of the
Old Testament.

Our Lord does not seem to have made use of the acted
parable, nor of the bold poetical imagery of the old prophets
and psalmists. It was no part of His method to rouse excitement in the minds of His hearers. There is nothing perhaps
which distinguishes His teaching from that of most popular
preachers and teachers more sharply than its calmness and
restraint. But His teaching was full of similes and parables.
Our earliest Gospel seems to say that His public teaching
consisted mainly of those charming and homely little word-
pictures drawn from the common life of the country folk,
each of which illustrated some aspect of the good tidings
which He came to impart. " Without a parable spake He not
unto them." His favourite opening was, " The kingdom of
Heaven is like . . ." In the Fourth Gospel we hear nothing
of parables. Their place is taken by symbolical expressions
in the form of metaphors, such as " I am the door," " I am
the good shepherd." The nature of God is described by
saying that " God is Spirit, God is Light, God is Love." The
word used by the evangelist for this symbolical language is
paroemia instead of *parabole*.

But there is one significant feature about our Lord's method
which is attested both by the synoptists and in the Fourth
Gospel. Our Lord had two methods of teaching, a direct and
an indirect. He had one method for the multitude and another

for His own disciples. In St. Matthew we read that His disciples came and said to Him, " Why speakest Thou unto them in parables ? " And He answered, " Unto you it is given to know the mysteries of the kingdom of heaven, but to them it is not given. For whosoever hath, to him shall be given, and he shall have more abundance ; but whosoever hath not, from him shall be taken away even that which he hath. Therefore speak I unto them in parables, because seeing they see not, and hearing they hear not, neither do they understand." So in St. John, our Lord tells His disciples that even His last discourses to them have been spoken in "proverbs", but that the hour cometh when He would no longer speak unto them in proverbs, but would show them plainly of the Father. This promise, like others of the same kind in the Gospel, is clearly meant to refer to the fuller understanding of our Lord's teaching which the disciples would obtain through the gift of the Holy Spirit, after His bodily presence had been withdrawn from them. Not only had much been said to the multitudes which could be fully understood only by the disciples, but much had been said to the disciples which could be fully understood by them only after the Spirit of Truth had come to guide them into all truth and to testify of Him. These discourses are in fact the message of the glorified Christ to the third generation of Christians.

The necessity for veiling the deepest part of His teaching is attributed by our Lord in the Synoptic Gospels to the moral and intellectual shortcomings of the multitude. He gives His teaching in an external symbolic form because no other was suited to His hearers. And afterwards He expounds everything to His disciples.

St. Matthew gives two examples of this private exposition, in the parables of the Sower and of the Tares of the field. Many, I think, must have felt surprise that explanations so simple as these should have been asked for by the disciples, and should have been withheld from the multitude. They are just what any intelligent person who had heard the parables would have gathered the interpretation to be, and they in no way answer the expectations aroused by the solemn words, " To you it is given to know the mysteries of the Kingdom of God." Either the parables in question were entirely thrown away on the multitude, or they gathered from them precisely those simple moral lessons which were afterwards given in plain language to the disciples. An obvious suggestion is that the Evangelist felt Himself at liberty to divulge these particular commentaries, just because they contained nothing esoteric. If our Lord used the phrase " the mysteries of the Kingdom of Heaven " in this connection, there must have been other teaching—so it has been suggested—which differed in kind as well as in form from that which formed the staple of His public discourses.

But it is very difficult to guess what this teaching could have been. If we are tempted to think that it may have resembled the Johannine handling of the Messianic hope, substituting virtually the coming of the Holy Spirit for the expected appearance of the Messiah in glory, we have to remember that the disciples did not assimilate this teaching, if it was ever given, and firmly believed that the return of their Master to earth would occur in the lifetime of some or all of them. The examples of His private discourses given by St. Matthew are far from suggesting such recondite and cryptic utterances as we find in some of the apocryphal sayings of Christ.

If we were dealing with a professed philosopher we might think otherwise. The prejudice against writing down the most intimate and precious parts of a doctrine was very strong in antiquity. Plato himself, if with most modern scholars we accept some of his Letters as genuine, has deprived us of that part of his message which he himself thought most valuable. I hope this is not so, but he more than hints at it. The notion of a *disciplina arcani* was fostered by the Gnostics, and then by the Alexandrians, both Christian and pagan. I need not trace the history of the alleged secret tradition in the Christian Church. It soon became a mere expedient for the defence of orthodox authority ; we cannot suppose that a syllable of our Lord's real teaching was handed down in this way.

This only we seem justified in saying, on the authority of the Gospels, that our Lord in some sort recognised the principle of reserve in imparting religious truth, and the necessity of giving it different forms in addressing different classes of people. It is also important that He sanctioned and used habitually the method of parable, that is, the dramatic presentation of spiritual lessons under forms easily understood. Our Lord must have been well aware that a price has to be paid for all picture-book theology, in the creation of illusions in the minds of the hearers which may easily stiffen into delusions and errors about matters of fact. The preacher who says, " The Kingdom of Heaven is like " is understood to mean, " The Kingdom of Heaven is." For example, the parable of the sheep and the goats is often mistaken for a description of the last judgment. Personally, I do not think He meant His language about His return in glory to be taken in the crude literal sense which His hearers gave to it. He taught His disciples practically nothing about the last judgment, heaven, and hell, that was not part of the popular belief among the Jews. This applies to the parable of Dives and Lazarus, and to the promise made to the penitent thief. He did not invent myths about the future, like Plato.

We have not gained much help towards solving our practical problem, by considering our Lord's method of teaching. The intellectual differences between the disciples and the multitude were after all not very great ; and our Lord had no esoteric

Gnosis to impart, such as Clement of Alexandria seems to have thought of. But as soon as scholars and thinkers entered the Church the conflict between them and the simple believers began. " Faith " and " Knowledge " became missiles, as they are to-day. As long as there is a sharp line of demarcation between the educated and the illiterate, the line of least resistance is to allow two types of religion, some kind of idealism for the educated, and superstitious institutionalism for the ignorant. There ought not to be this sharp line, by which religion and philosophy both suffered. Platonism was much injured by the practice of teaching a crude dualism to the vulgar, as an explanation of the evil in the world, while reserving more refined speculations for the inner circle.

In the Middle Ages the prevailing illiteracy and the practice of writing in Latin secured scholars against the perils and attractions of a reading public. There was no reading public. Popular religion was a mass of gross superstitions, with their centre in sacerdotal magic, while the divines were writing ponderous works on systematic theology, and the mystics were exploring the highest regions of religious experience. During the whole of the Middle Ages there was no conflict between religion and science such as we are familiar with. Science was almost dead, and theology was quite abreast with the philosophy of the time, which indeed was studied mainly by ecclesiastics.

This restriction of religious thought to a small class of scholars is now quite impossible. An enormous mass of half-educated readers constitutes a new and very serious difficulty. No one who now writes a book knows into whose hands it will fall ; and even a sermon or address intended for students is likely to appear in the daily press, strangely distorted and absurdly divided by staring headlines, representing possibly the theology of the sub-editor, but not that of the writer.

Many men who have a message are silenced by the fear of doing more harm than good by publishing it. In a democratic community the half-educated decide what may and may not be said, and scholars naturally withdraw themselves from this kind of censorship.

Our worst difficulties are inherited from the time of the Renaissance. The age of the great schoolmen was over before the discoveries of Copernicus presented the Church with the gravest problem which it has had to face since the European-ising of the Gospel which began with St. Paul. The descent into Hades; the resuscitation of the material body of the Crucified and its transportation to the heavenly places where God dwells; the return through the clouds; the ascent of the souls of men reunited with their bodies; the subterranean dungeons of the wicked; the spirits, good and bad, who flit about in the upper regions of the air—all this fell into its place in the pre-Copernican universe, and was believed in as scientific fact. By no ingenuity can all of it be fitted into the framework of the universe as for nearly four hundred years we have known it to be. The Church of the Renaissance forced Galileo to retract, wrongly, as we all believe; but the implica-tions of Copernican astronomy in the field of dogma have never been faced and are hardly being faced to-day.

Compared with this unhealed wound, more recent dis-coveries, such as the doctrine of evolution, the ascent of man from lower animal types, the antiquity of our globe, and all the results of Biblical and historical criticism, are unimportant. The great question at issue between science and theology is four hundred years old. The scientific doctrine which de-stroyed the traditional cosmology has long been an undisputed fact; but the necessary readjustment of beliefs is not taken in hand, because the Church is ruled by half-educated Christians, and by ecclesiastics who feel their pulse.

There is no reason whatever to think that our Lord wished to strew intellectual difficulties in the way of His followers. His demands in the ethical sphere are stern enough. We are bidden to follow Him in the path which leads to Calvary. But assuredly He did not require us to outrage our scientific conscience as a condition of being His disciples. These burdens, grievous to be borne, are not part of the burden of the Cross. They are laid on the shoulders of men and women by our scribes and lawyers, and they hinder many who wish to take up their cross as our Master bade us.

As a recent writer has said, " The history of the ecclesiastical persecution of honest thinkers is just one illustration of what Hilary of Poitiers called *irreligiosa sollicitudo pro Deo*. Galileo forced to abjure his beliefs and thrown into prison, Servetus and Giordano Bruno burned at the stake, Buffon compelled to retract his hypotheses, Colenso excommunicated, Maurice and Robertson Smith deprived of their Professorships—so it goes on from generation to generation." This writer quotes from a newspaper of a hundred years ago. " Such things as railroads and telegraphs are impossibilities and rank infidelity. There is nothing in the Word of God about them. If God had designed that His intelligent creatures should travel at the frightful speed of fifteen miles an hour, he would have foretold it through His Holy Prophets. It is a device of Satan to lead immortal souls down to Hell."

There is no reason for hard words or hard thoughts on either side. There are some, it seems, who have really persuaded themselves that there is a conspiracy of traitors who wish to break up the Christian faith by betraying the fortress from within. What possible motive could there be for such a plot ? Ambition and self-seeking would never prompt a man to be a liberal theologian. It is no joke to excite the rage of furious ecclesiastics. There are no doubt some students who forget the deep and vital interests which in the minds of many are intertwined with the historical and scientific problems which they discuss; but even they should be acquitted of any sinister intention. Most of those who wish to see the shackles of tradition relaxed are only conscious of the injustice and folly of compelling men and women in the twentieth century to live in a pre-Copernican universe. They think that the truth should make us free, as free as those can be who are pledged to bring every thought into captivity to the obedience of Christ.

But on the other side, charges of obscurantism should not be lightly brought. A readjustment of traditional dogma is a very delicate and difficult operation, and the rulers of a great Church cannot disregard the convictions and prejudices of those who are content with the faith of their grandmother Lois and their mother Eunice. I honestly think that we are now allowed a very reasonable liberty, for which we ought to be thankful.

But I have something more to say to our so-called modernists. Can we really escape from the law that while we live on earth all our knowledge must be largely symbolic? Take, for instance, the scientific view of the world, which claims to be coherent and all-embracing, and sometimes demands that all religious beliefs should be brought under its categories. Science has proved the soundness of its working hypotheses by a career of uninterrupted and brilliant success. But would it not be true to say that science, for its own purposes, disregards a whole range of higher values, all the imponderables which make up the best part of human life? If we believe, as the religious man does believe, that these ultimate and eternal values are the most real things in our experience; that they are not merely ideals, but the highest order of facts, the creative and living thoughts of God who made the world and all things that are therein, can we be satisfied with a theory of the universe which aims at a complete explanation of reality without these values ; which classifies things by their roots and not by their fruits, and often forgets how much of the world as known to science is really a mental construction, based itself on a valuation, and that a very imperfect one ? All the external world is but a symbol, a parable, a figure of the true. It can teach us much, but not everything. " Every truth," said Isaac Pennington, " is shadow except the last ; but every truth is substance in its own place, though it be but a shadow in another place. And the shadow is a true shadow, as the substance is a true substance." All life is sacramental, full of divine meanings. We are all trying to find bridges between the world of fact and the world of value. Let us be gentle with each other, for we are all very much in the dark together.

I am sure that philosophers cannot escape from these limitations. Let us suppose that we have found some great school of thought intellectually satisfying. When we try to realise its doctrines, and to make them a home for our living faith and hope and love, am I wrong in saying that they begin at once to take a parabolic form ? The eternal above time is translated into unending duration ; pictures of a local habitation of blessed spirits come back unbidden ; the spiritual mode of existence is immobilised into a statuesque inactivity, or travestied as an endless repetition of futile performances. Our imagination restores just those parables which we thought we had left behind. I think there is some truth in the maxim *Lex Orandi Lex Credendi.* If our aim is to " see the invisible " we may use whatever spectacles seem to suit our eyesight best.

These thoughts should suggest humility and tolerance even of the intolerant. But the obligation remains to offer to God our best science and our best philosophy. We shall not correct the limitations of scientific truth by mixing it with scientific falsehood, nor imitate the great religious pioneers of the first century by refusing to question any tradition of the elders.

The recognition that God teaches us by parables in no way implies that there is no such thing as absolute truth, or that it must be always beyond our reach. Indeed, I think it implies just the contrary. If there were no absolute truth, there would be no symbols ; if there were no substance there would be no shadows. Now we see as in a mirror, through symbols, but then face to face ; now I know in part, but then shall I know even as also I am known. Let us follow the Greek fathers who called the life and death and resurrection of Christ a sacrament or mystery, a revelation of the path which we all must tread, the death unto sin which we all must die, the " rising with Christ", and the ascension with Him "in heart and mind " which we hope will at last admit us to the realm where God will no more " speak to us in proverbs", "for we shall see Him as He is."

CHAPTER IX

THE JUSTICE OF GOD

SHALL not the Judge of all the earth do right? So asks Abraham near the beginning of our Bible, and has no doubt of the answer. Certainly, if there be a God, He must be a righteous God; for the idea of God includes the idea of righteousness; an unrighteous God would not be God—if He were indifferent, we should call Him natural law; if malignant, the Devil. Further, if there be a God, He must govern the world, for that too is contained in the idea of God. A God who did not govern the world would be no concern of ours. And yet we do not find that the world is governed in accordance with our ideas of justice. Hence the problem.

A great many solutions have been proposed. The Epicurean thought that the gods did not *care*—they lived their own life and took no interest in our affairs. Asiatic thought has often had recourse to *dualism*—a just and righteous God struggling not very successfully against a hostile, malignant Power. But a limited, struggling God would not be God, but only a Spirit among other spirits. If the good and the evil Spirit are wrestling in the arena, who is the umpire? The umpire must be some over-God; and we have then to consider how *He* can be just. No solution which denies God's omnipotence can be satisfactory. Others have said, The battle is still raging, but the issue is certain and preordained. This, I hope, is true; but it raises other questions. If injustice continues to the end of the battle, and is only put down at the last, have all those who lived and died during the conflict got the justice which they had a right to expect from omnipotence? And what will be the state of things when the battle is over ? Will justice triumph in this world, or must we call into existence a new earth to redress the balance of the old ? Must we transfer justice to some far-distant sphere, or to some ideal world of the imagination ? Must we admit that injustice is the rule here on earth—that Dives lives and dies happy, laden with undeserved blessings, while Lazarus is as miserable as he appears to be—and then believe that as in the parable (for it *is* a parable, and not a description of the next world, of which our Lord as man willed to know nothing), compensation in kind is paid and exacted, Dives being tormented and Lazarus comforted, not so much by way of moral retribution as to make their accounts square in the matter of pleasures and pains ? No ! eternity *is* an essential factor in what we are to believe about Divine justice ; but not this crude notion of compensation in kind.

Another favourite solution, more popular in antiquity than in modern times, is that the individual is not the unit to whom justice is done. The unit may be the family, or the nation. The family or nation in which some great crime has been committed is pursued by a hereditary curse. Or else the family dies out ; the evil man leaves no descendants—no children prattle round his knees, as Homer says. Or, since the mills of God grind slowly, the doom strikes the family of the malefactor in the third or fourth generation.

Others have thought to justify the ways of God to man by attacking the notion of evil itself. Does evil touch the good man at all ? Can we not see, in what appears to be evil, the necessary means by which the world-order is evolved ? Cannot we consent to the decrees of nature, or God, whatever they are, and make them our own ? So argued the Stoics. " I do nothing under compulsion," says Seneca ; " I do not obey God slavishly. I freely consent with Him, knowing that all things happen by fixed laws." " Those whom God loves,

G

He hardens and braces and disciplines; He loves the good with a manly love, and says to them, Let them be disciplined by labour, pain, and loss, that they may acquire true strength." " A spectacle worthy of God is a brave man struggling with adversity." We have here two topics of consolation blended. Pain and loss are not evils, but wholesome discipline. And he who can rationally and devoutly assent to the universal law can find nothing in the course of nature to regret.

The American philosopher Emerson goes even further than the Stoics. He argues that justice is done universally, here and now, if we could only see it. It is only on a base estimate of what makes happiness that the bad are happy and the good miserable. From a higher point of view, all things are moral. Justice is not postponed. Crime and punishment grow out of one stem. Punishment is a fruit which ripens unsuspected within the flower of the pleasure which concealed it. You cannot do wrong without suffering wrong. The thief steals from himself; the swindler swindles himself. Nothing can work me damage except myself. I am never a real sufferer but by my own fault.

Lastly, there have been some who have given up all attempt to explain the mystery, and have fallen back on blind faith. " For the just man," says Plato, " all things will at last work together for good, both in life and in death."

We find most of these theories in the Bible. The Old Testament writers try and reject one after another. " The sins of the fathers are visited on the children." " No," cries Ezekiel ; " ye shall no more have occasion to use this proverb in Israel. The son shall not bear the iniquity of the father. The soul that sinneth, it shall die." " I have been young, and now am old ; yet never saw I the righteous forsaken," says one Psalmist. " Nay," says Ecclesiastes, " there is one event to the righteous and to the wicked." " In the next generation shall his name be clean put out," says one. " Nay," says another, " the wicked have children at their desire, and leave the rest of their substance to their babes."

So great is the perplexity ; so inextinguishable the hope and faith ; so grievous the disappointment.

The whole problem is dealt with in Job. Had the sufferer committed secret sins ? Were his sufferings only a passing trial ? Both these are rejected. Then shall he take an attitude of dumb resignation ? Shall he say, " Behold, I am of small account, what shall I answer thee ? I lay my hand upon my mouth, I will not answer." Are the glories of nature a sufficient make-weight for the miseries of man ? Is the Maker of Leviathan and Behemoth, of the Pleiades and Orion, too great to be called to account because a good man loses his all and is tormented by loathsome disease ? The book gives no answer ; for the restoration of Job's fortune, with a new wife and family, is little better than an ironical conclusion.

In Daniel and the second Isaiah we find the hope of personal immortality arising like a day-star in the darkness. And in Isaiah liii we have for the first time the noble thought that the sufferings of the innocent have a wider than individual meaning—that they have a healing power for the whole nation.

In the light of a fuller revelation, we cannot feel that the treatment of the problem in the Old Testament is satisfactory. The Hebrews, like other Semitic peoples, did not understand justice as we do. Justice or righteousness does not in the Old Testament (except in a very few instances) convey the idea of a nicely adjusted scale of reward and punishment. Such an idea was foreign to their experience. They naturally conceived of God after the pattern of the kings whom they knew—Oriental chiefs or sultans. It is not " injustice " for such princes to be arbitrary and capricious. It is expected of them, and their subjects may be thankful if they preserve some moderation in the exercise of their undoubted rights. There was nothing shocking to them in the most flagrant disproportion between guilt and penalty. The writer who describes the killing of Uzzah for touching the ark, must have conceived of the " holiness " of Jehovah as something more like electricity than any moral quality.

It is indeed remarkable how late a development is the horror of disproportionate severity. Consider the favourite plots of Greek tragedy—the relentless punishments of the gods for some venial act of pride. Think of Prometheus crucified for a generous error—Christianity is all on the side of Prometheus against Zeus.

We have no right to be surprised, for our criminal law, till within living memory, was as blazing an example of disproportionate severity as can be found in any Greek or Eastern stories. Listen for one minute to British " justice " in 1818. I have copied the official record of the Lincolnshire assizes in that year :

A retired soldier ; entering a house and stealing a coat and jacket. Death.

A boy of 15 ; breaking open a desk and stealing £1 3s. 6d. Death.

A boy of 17 ; entering a house with intent to steal. Death.

Two young men ; housebreaking. Death.

A boy of 19 ; firing an oat stack. Death.

Two young men for the same offence. Death.

Two boys for burglary. Death.

A man of 30 ; for entering a shop and stealing a pair of shoes. Death.

This callousness has an important bearing on the doctrine of future punishment, which we have inherited from times when stupid, senseless cruelty of this kind excited no surprise or reprobation. Such as men themselves are, such they will imagine God to be. Human justice is modelled on our ideas of Divine justice. The modern revolt against the dreadful pictures of hell which we have inherited is inevitable and amply justified.

But let us turn from theories to the world as we know it. What seems to be the truth about justice in this world?

We should prefer a world in which poetical justice was done, as it is in old-fashioned fiction; though here also we are less fierce than the early Victorians. I recall a novel in which an atheist is swallowed up in molten lead, falling on his hands in the first instance; and another in which a Jesuit is eaten by rats in a secret passage of his own contrivance. We forget sometimes how absolutely our Lord condemned this kind of thing. A tower, whether in Siloam or London, is not at all more likely to fall because criminals or atheists happen to be walking under it.

Many clergymen and moralists think that they are doing God service by drawing lurid pictures of the punishments with which Nature visits vice. The plain truth is that Nature has no diseases ready for the worst scoundrels. She punishes the drunkard, and in a very random and blind manner the less heinous forms of impurity. The most horrible offences under this head entail no physical danger. It is therefore absolutely indefensible to use the blind cruelty of nature to reinforce the motives for clean living.

The law of heredity has been shorn of much of its moral force. Acquired tendencies are probably not transmitted, so that except by bad example a father is not liable by his misconduct to taint the character of his son.

Nature has a morality, but her methods are rude and clumsy. She trusts to us to rectify them in dealing with our fellow-men.

But what a false abstraction it is to speak of Nature apart from humanity! Humanity is part of Nature. Our reasoning faculties which enable us to conquer Nature by obeying her,

are part of Nature. Our affection for our fellow-men, our
sense of justice, our sense of pity, our self-respect, which makes
us abhor things which our lower appetites desire, our belief
in a heavenly Father who can hear our prayers—all these
things are a part of Nature. They have a right to be there ;
God made them, as He made the world.

Nature apart from man knows nothing of human justice ;
but then Nature is not apart from man. God has never promised that the world shall be just to man when men are unjust
to each other. This is a good world for us because God has
given us the great privilege of making it better. That is why
God has implanted in us the sense of justice, the love of fair
play, and generous indignation at the sight of wrong. The
historical answer to the pious wish, " God mend all," was,
" Nay, then, we must help Him to mend it."

The problem of individual justice doubtless remains on our
hands. But let us not have any *meum* and *tuum* account with
our Maker. God's justice is done rather by the transformation
of ourselves than of our circumstances, and this is what we
really desire. If it is His will that we should be admitted to a
share in Christ's unmerited sufferings "for his body's sake",
shall we make that a grievance ? " For hereunto were we
called ; because Christ also suffered for us, leaving us an
example that we should follow his steps. Who, when he was
reviled, reviled not again ; when he suffered, he threatened
not ; but committed himself to him that judgeth righteously."
Shall not the Judge of all the earth do right ? Yes, verily ;
though He slay me, yet will I trust in Him.

CHAPTER X

WAR

IN the early part of the war a young English officer, who was killed on the following day, wrote his last letter to his father :

" Having been about all night digging, I was shifted to make room for some other company. I advanced to a cemetery to defend it and stayed there most of the day. It is a beastly thing to have to do, digging trenches among graves and pulling down crosses and ornamental wreaths to make room. One feels that something is wrong when a man lies down behind a child's grave to shoot at a bearded German who has probably got a family anxiously awaiting his return at home. It was a miserable day, wet, and spent in a cemetery under those conditions. There was a large crucifix at one end. The sight of the bullets chipping Christ's image about, and the knowledge of what He has done for us and the Germans, and what we were doing to His consecrated ground and each other, made one feel sick of the whole war, or sicker than before."

The men at the front "felt that something was wrong", and sometimes said so in plain words, like this poor boy. I think most of us feel it now. We all learnt in our childhood Southey's poem about the Battle of Blenheim, with the child's unanswered and unanswerable question, " And what good came of it at last ? " said little Wilhelmine. " The wrath of man worketh not the righteousness of God." We knew it, of course, and I never met anyone who wished for war, with

Germany or any other country; but we are told, perhaps
rightly—it is not for me to say—that the country must fight,
that there was no help for it. The people of the other belliger-
ent countries were told the same; and so millions of men,
who a week before were absorbed in their peaceful work and
play in their quiet homes, with their families round them, were
hurled against each other for four years of scientific butchery.
We need not now apportion the guilt. It is as Europeans, as
Christians, as civilised men, that we are all called to penitence,
a penitence in which we may find the path to reconciliation.

The young officer's words recall that unforgettable para-
graph in *Sartor Resartus* :

" There dwell and live in the British village of Dumdrudge
some 500 souls. From these, by certain natural enemies of the
French, there are selected during the French war, say, 30 able-
bodied men. Dumdrudge, at her own expense, has suckled
and nursed them; she has, not without difficulty and sorrow,
fed them up to manhood, and even trained them to crafts, so
that one can weave and another build, another hammer.
Nevertheless, among much weeping and swearing, they are
selected, all dressed in red, and shipped away at the public
charges, say to the south of Spain, and kept there till they are
wanted. And now to that same spot in the south of Spain are
30 similar French artisans, from a French Dumdrudge, in like
manner wending; till at length the two parties come into
actual juxtaposition, and 30 stand fronting 30, each with a gun
in his hand. Straightway the word ' Fire ' is given, and they
blow the souls out of one another; and in place of 60 brisk,
useful craftsmen the world has 60 dead carcasses, which it
must bury and shed tears for. Had these men any quarrel?
Busy as the devil is, not the smallest. They lived far enough
apart; were the entirest strangers; nay, in so wide a universe,

there was even unconsciously, by commerce, some mutual helpfulness between them."

The war, while it lasted, seemed to us to have been caused by the deliberate wickedness of an abstract demon called Germany. The Germans were more or less honestly persuaded that similar abstractions called Russia, France, and England were the criminals. Now it seems to most of us that we were all stark mad together. The chief obstacle to penitence is, indeed, the suspicion that none of the parties concerned were responsible for their actions.

The utter futility and folly of modern war had often been demonstrated. Wars are waged, I suppose, for territory, or for plunder, or for trade. As for the first, nothing weakens a country more than unwilling subjects. As for indemnities, I have it on good authority that Bismarck declared that if he made another successful war, one of the terms of peace would be that Germany should pay a large indemnity to the losers. As for trade, if our most energetic competitor and our best customer happen to own the same head, it is not good business to cut that head off. And let anyone estimate the value to us of the tropics and all the blacks who inhabit them and compare the total with what the war has cost us. A sane man does not pay two thousand pounds a year in fire insurance for a haystack.

I cannot admit that to demonstrate the economic lunacy of war is to appeal to " low motives." That is sheer cant. National bankruptcy means widespread unemployment, children with pinched faces and legs like broomsticks ; it means civil war and revolution ; it means the relapse of civilisation into barbarism, since it is the most highly educated classes, as we see everywhere in Europe, who are first ruined.

Well, perhaps the business community will not again make the mistake of thinking that war can ever be good business. Even the Press, I am told, has found that it is very bad business, from its point of view. But the liability to attacks of war fever is so great and the irrationality of human beings so intractable that we cannot rely on appeals to common sense. The moral appeal must come first, if for no other reason, because the war spirit makes a successful appeal to the idealist as well as to the self-regarding. As Canon Grane says, it was the moral effect of an obscure monk's self-sacrifice which brought the bloody games of the Coliseum to an end. And the emancipation of the slaves was won, not by proving that free labour would produce more sugar and more cotton than the cowhide lash, but by persuading public opinion that slavery as an institution involved horrors which were an outrage on humanity and an insult to God.

The moral appeal just now must mainly take the form of penitence and the spirit of reconciliation. Europe has deep cause for penitence. Do we realise these two things : first, that the relations of civilised mankind had become so close that this war was at least as much a civil war as the chronic wars between the various cantons of ancient Greece ? And, secondly, that after a century of growing humanity, a century which prided itself on having banished cruelty from the statute books, and which even concerned itself in safeguarding the rights of the lower animals to decent treatment, the nations of Europe were no sooner locked in the death-grapple than horrors and atrocities were committed which ten, or a hundred, or even two thousand years ago, would have been thought incredible except in savage warfare ? If this seems to you too strong, let me quote to you a few sentences from the Republic of Plato, in which Socrates lays down what seem to him to be reasonable and practicable rules for the conduct of war between Greek states. I have just said that the civilised world is quite as much bound together by common traditions and habits and convictions as were the Greek states, so that the comparison is a fair one.

"Do you think it right," asks Socrates, "that Greeks should enslave Greeks, considering the danger that all Greece is in of barbarian conquest? Clearly, no Greek should make a slave of another Greek. Then we must abstain from spoiling the dead or hindering their burial. Neither shall we offer up trophies in the temples of the gods, fearing that the offering of trophies taken from kinsmen may be a pollution. Again, we shall not devastate the land of Greek enemies, nor burn their houses; it is only lawful to reap standing corn and take it for ourselves, without injuring the next harvest." This is pagan war morality 2300 years ago. Think of this, you who have seen North-Eastern France. And now it is widely assumed that if there is another war each side will try to exterminate the women and children of the other by poison! I cannot altogether account for this outbreak of diabolism. But while such things are done and justified, the less we talk about progress the better.

This reversion to savagery is not mainly the result of the new inventions. It is as easy to murder a child with a spear or club as with a bomb. But till the Great War such things were not done.

In part, no doubt, these horrors are the result of the elaborately engineered propaganda of hatred which all the belligerents employed, knowing that the average man needs some incitement to kill his fellow-man. This is one of the most devilish parts of the whole business. The soldiers were told untrue stories of the outrages committed by the other side. Furious hatred and indignation were artificially stimulated. Even religion was freely dragged in. One side appealed to their " good old ally, God "; the other represented the war as " a struggle between Corsica and Calvary." Alas, the

spirit of the Corsican was not hovering over one army only !
So the minds of the belligerents were systematically poisoned
by their own governments, and the deadly spirit of hatred
thus generated has been slow to subside. To quote Canon
Grane again : " Long after Nature has hidden with her kindly
cloak the ghastly evidence of inhuman strife, the unseen spirit
of war-engendered hate continues to embitter the national
heart, exciting rancour in the defeated and arrogance in the
victorious, poisoning in both the natural wells of fraternity
and peace."

And then we think of the peace. The victors had to consider whether they wished to make an end of war, knowing,
as we all know, that another war in our time would destroy
our civilisation utterly ; or whether they wished to make a
vindictive peace, which the losers would think themselves more
than justified in tearing up at the first opportunity. If we
wished the former, we ought to have offered the Germans
terms which they themselves would have thought unexpectedly
generous, and then to have said to them, " Now we have given
you no excuse for plotting revenge ; join us in establishing a
League of Nations and universal disarmament, and let us all
help each other to gather up the fragments that remain." We
say that the Germans showed no sign of repentance. Did we
make it easy for them to repent ? The human heart is like
water : it freezes at a certain temperature, and melts under the
influence of warmth. The Christian method is to overcome
evil with good. It does not always succeed ; but the opposite
method, of driving out devils by Beelzebub, invariably fails.

So far as I can gather from those who have travelled in
Germany, the Germans were rather less bitter and fierce than
we should be if we had met with the same treatment. But I
should not like to build upon this, I have no wish to talk
politics ; I merely point out the obvious fact that if one of a

pair of gamblers has won and exacted full payment of a heavy stake, and then says, " Now we will play for love for the rest of the evening," his proposal is not likely to find favour with the loser.

It is an appalling state of things ; and what should our feelings be when we turn to our Bibles, to the visions of the prophets and the promise of the Incarnation. " O that thou hadst hearkened to my law ! Then had thy peace been as a river, and thy righteousness as the waves of the sea." The crowning title of the coming deliverer in Isaiah's prophecy was the Prince of Peace. " Of the increase of his government, and peace, there shall be no end." " Nation shall not lift up sword against nation, neither shall they learn war any more." The happy vision seemed to be near its fulfilment in the angels' song, " Glory to God in the highest, and on earth peace, good-will toward men." Alas ! another passage in the Gospels comes to our minds : " If thou hadst known, even thou, in this thy day, the things that belong to thy peace ; but now they are hid from thine eyes."

But, if it please God, it is not yet too late. The gate of repentance is not yet shut. We have all sinned and suffered together ; we may all repent together. We may help to bear one another's burdens ; not only by relieving the necessities of those who are suffering most, but by bearing one another's moral burdens. But here a caution is needed. We English are a sentimental people ; and some of us, in our reaction from the hatred fostered during the war, and our shame at having given way to the absurd idea that every one who has had the misfortune to be born between the Rhine and the Vistula has a double dose of original sin, have rushed to the opposite extreme, and speak as if the Germans were amiable and injured innocents. That will not do at all. They have at least as much to repent of as we have—indeed, I still think they have more ; but we must help them to show their best selves by showing them our best selves.

Justice, common sense, and good-will are the qualities which are needed, not sentimentality. The spirit of civilisation would say to us all, " Sirs, ye are brethren ; why do ye wrong one to another ? " We are brethren, we Europeans ; if one member suffers, all the members suffer with it. We have discovered this to our great cost in the economic sphere ; we must learn it also in the moral sphere. We cannot afford a humiliated, embittered and degenerate Germany any more than a triumphant militarist Germany. The harmony of the European symphony needs the best notes of all its members. And who after all are the typical Germans—Goethe, Schiller, Kant, Beethoven, or the Slavs Nietzsche and Treitschke and the Englishman Houston Stewart Chamberlain ?

" If ye forgive not men their trespasses, neither will your Father in heaven forgive your trespasses."

" Repent ye therefore and be converted, that your sins may be blotted out, when the times of refreshing shall come from the presence of the Lord."

CHAPTER XI

WAR*

IT is a great privilege and a great responsibility to preach at Geneva at the annual meeting of this august body, to which the whole world looks to find some remedy for the worst disease of civilisation—war and the ever-present danger of war. It is a great privilege and responsibility, it is also a very difficult task that has been laid upon me. You do not wish to hear platitudes about the blessings of peace and the almost unthinkable horrors which another war would bring upon humanity. We are all agreed that Christ came to bring peace on earth, and that wars between the nations who have accepted His Gospel are a scandal. But there is a strange inertia in the public mind. Even thoughtful and religious people are not sufficiently alive either to the peril which hangs over civilisation or to the flagrant contradiction between the condition of international politics and the principles of Christianity. But you who hear me to-day all know these things very well ; you do not need any pulpit oratory to remind you of them.

On the other hand, if the preacher takes all these things for granted, and tries to offer something definite and constructive, he is fortunate if he avoids making suggestions which those who have for years been engaged on the practical work of the League have already considered and found impracticable. He may also, if he is not very careful, seem to be imputing blame to one or another of the Great Powers, who may seem to him, in his ignorance, to be placing their own security, or their

* A Sermon preached in the Cathedral of St. Pierre, Geneva, on the occasion of the Ninth Assembly of the League of Nations.

desire to avoid foreign entanglements, above the common interests of the civilised world. The nations must bear one another's burdens, and eschew fault-finding. The unruly wills and affections of sinful men are the material on which the League has to work. But since there is not the slightest doubt that in every country all except an infinitesimal minority earnestly desire to see war banished from the earth, it would be faithless to doubt that some way of carrying into effect what the whole world desires may in time be found. In time, I say, for it is a race between common sense and overwhelming catastrophe. The books of the Sibyl will not always be for sale.

I do not think it is at all helpful to inveigh against the wickedness and folly of human nature in general, still less against the wickedness and folly of particular nations or particular classes. The out-and-out pacifist—you must forgive me for saying it—is usually a rather naïve and ill-informed person, convinced of his own rectitude and ready to denounce imaginary wicked people, whom he calls militarists, imperialists, diplomats, aristocrats, emperors or what not and whom he supposes to be naturally bloodthirsty and indifferent to the sufferings which their insensate ambition causes to the innocent masses. I believe that such denunciations do unmitigated harm, and are a serious hindrance to the work of the League. I shall therefore take leave to contradict them, before passing on to what seem to me to be the real sources of danger.

Civilised nations do not regard war as a sport, they do not enjoy fighting as the head-hunting tribes of Borneo are said to do. Nor is it true that wars are made by the manufacturers of armaments or by groups of financiers. The influence of such trades and groups is not great ; and Big Business has far more to lose than to gain by a general conflagration.

The notion that wars are made only by kings and emperors, and that to make the world safe for democracy is to make it safe for peace, is utterly untrue, and extremely dangerous. The old proverb, *Delirant reges, plectuntur Achivi*, requires to be amended in the light of recent events. It should run *Delirant Achivi, plectuntur reges*. Nations go mad and make scape-goats of their rulers. My study of modern history convinces me that in bellicosity and injustice to weaker nations there is not a pin to choose between monarchies and republics.

There is unfortunately rather more justification for the charge that some wars have been wars of exploitation—economic wars. These are always attacks by some great power on barbarous or ill-armed nations. This is precisely the kind of war which the League of Nations ought to be able to prevent. As for wars between great nations on the same level of civilisation, like the Great War of 1914, we may surely say without fear of contradiction that no one who has anything to lose is ever likely to vote for such a war again. Frankly, I regard this as the trump card in the hands of the friends of peace. It gives the opponents of war a most potent argument which they have never been able to use with such convincing force before.

As for those persons, and I fear they are numerous, who wish to abolish international rivalries only in order to clear the way for a ruthless and probably sanguinary civil war of classes in the bosom of every nation, the friends of peace may pray to be delivered from such allies. In that direction lies a deadly menace to the whole movement.

Having thus to the best of my ability deprecated some of the mistaken diagnoses and unhelpful remedies which too often darken counsel in this great problem, let me try to suggest to you what are the real causes which place serious obstacles to the triumph of the cause which we all have at heart.

H

The first of these is the form which the spirit of patriotism has taken in modern times.

The love of country has burnt with a peculiarly intense flame in the time in which we live. There have been times when the privileged classes in different countries have felt more sympathetic with each other than with the masses in their own country. This sympathy mitigated patriotic ardour in the eighteenth century. Earlier in history, the international Catholic Church disputed the national allegiance of Europeans. The Church prevented some wars and made others; but the wars were seldom national in the modern sense. But ever since the French Revolution and Napoleon kindled into a fierce flame the national consciousness which they wished to extinguish, patriotism has been by far the strongest of the generous emotions which make the European man ready to sacrifice his property and his life, without counting the cost. In its dangerous form it is the aftermath of Romanticism. The European has idealised his own country, almost personifying or deifying it. He has invested it with every glorious attribute; he has persuaded himself that his countrymen, collectively, are the salt of the earth; he has pictured for it a grandiose destiny as the pioneer of a higher and nobler civilisation than the world has yet seen. To extend this *Kultur* over the whole earth, to take up the " White Man's burden " for the benefit of the " lesser breeds "; perhaps even to restore for one's own nationals the Empire of Charlemagne, of Augustus, or of the Greek Emperors—such are the megalomaniac dreams that have floated before the minds of several great nations in our time.

Are we to join those who condemn outright these sentiments of love, pride and devotion which for very many persons are the one unselfish passion which they are able to cherish? Have we found that those who are ostentatiously free from them, those who are sometimes the friends and advocates of every country except their own, are morally superior, more worthy of respect, than the romantic imperialist? I think not. And yet this megalomaniac nationalism is one of the chief causes of war, and it is all the more dangerous because when roused to enthusiasm it disregards those considerations of loss and gain which to men like Norman Angell seem so conclusive. To the patriot in an exalted mood the questions at issue between his own country and its enemies seem to be simply questions of right against wrong; to count the cost and estimate the danger seems a mean and unworthy thing. We know, alas, how when the sword has once been drawn, every government tries to stimulate these prejudices by unscrupulous propaganda, and how when terms of peace are to be discussed, hatred and indignation, thus artificially exaggerated, stifle the desire to show justice and generosity to a beaten foe, which enlightened self-interest no less than chivalry and Christian charity should encourage. In this way a passionate wish for a war of revenge is generated in the minds of the losers, and each war sows the seeds of another.

But this sentiment of patriotism is far too noble a thing to be condemned outright. It needs only to be directed into right channels, to be purified from its base, vulgar and archaic perversions. The question is not whether we ought to love our country, but what kind of success and glory and happiness we should desire for it. Instead of the childish wish to paint the map of the world red, or whatever our national colour may be, our pride should be to make it honoured, respected and even beloved by other nations. A nation is honoured in the world for its contributions to literature, art, science and political wisdom. It is honoured also for any acts of international generosity, of which there are unfortunately not many examples, but which have not been unknown in modern history. Instances of such generosity are the help which France and England gave to Greece and Italy in their struggle for freedom and national unity, and the grant of independence to Cuba by the United States. Nations are not incapable of gratitude; the very rarity of disinterested action by a government increases the effect of an act of generosity.

This duty of elevating and purifying the love of country should come home to every citizen individually. We can all take our part in forming public opinion. We can all reprove and discountenance every manifestation of vulgar arrogance, of indifference to the rights of the weak, every mean and poor aim for our country. We can all show that we " covet earnestly the best gifts " for it ; and we can all help to turn dislike and jealousy of foreign nations into that kind of sporting emulation in which we meet, with friendly rivalry, the champions of a rival college, university or county, in the cricket or football field. You remember the words of Marcus Aurelius. The poet says : " Dear City of Cecrops." Shall not I say : " Dear City of God " ? Christ, who wept over Jerusalem, will not reprove the most passionate patriotism, if the vision which inspires it is that of a country founded on love and justice. " Without justice," says Augustine, " an empire is only a gang of robbers."

Romantic patriotism, which is only the distortion of a noble sentiment, is one of the causes of modern war. But the main cause is simply fear—fear of sudden and unprovoked attack. And here again we must beware of passing thoughtless censure. The plain truth is that the fear is justified. As Theodore Roosevelt said : " It is idle to make speeches and write essays against this fear, because at present the fear has a real basis. At present each nation has cause for the fear it feels. Each nation has cause to believe that its national life is in peril unless it is able to take the national life of one or more of its

foes, or at least hopelessly to cripple that foe. The causes of
fear must be removed, or no matter what peace may be patched
up to-day or what new treaties may be negotiated to-morrow,
these causes will at some future day bring about the same
results, bring about a repetition of the same awful tragedy."
I need not point out to you how fear drove all the chief
belligerents in the Great War to take up arms. In our own
case the one convincing and unanswerable argument was that
of the Prime Minister : " If we remain neutral we shall be left
without a friend in the world, the predestined victims of the
next coalition."

I have named the two chief causes of war, but no doubt
there is a third. The government of a country may see that
the nation is disintegrating and heading for civil strife. An
appeal to patriotism, to defend the country against a foreign
enemy, may seem to be the only chance of averting internal
disruption. It can hardly be doubted that this argument did
weigh with more than one government in 1914. The conse-
quences, however, were so disastrous that it seems very
unlikely that this gambler's stake will be played again.

We are left, therefore, with two causes which I mentioned
first—patriotism and fear. Can this League of Nations remove
the well-grounded fears of the nations that they may be
attacked and destroyed without provocation ? Hitherto, un-
warlike nations have found no mercy. We need only think of
the treatment of China all through the nineteenth century.
Or must we go on as we have done hitherto, each nation
naturally desiring to be secure, and realising that it cannot be
secure unless it is stronger than any probable assailant ? This
is surely the crux of the whole problem. Can the League offer
the nations security, not against nations which are willing to
keep the Covenant, but against any nation which may choose
to break it ? I have no doubt that this question is constantly

before the minds of the Council of the League and of the numerous publicists in Europe and America who realise the situation. It would ill become me to advocate any particular solution; I have not the requisite knowledge. Whether the suggestion of an international air force is worth serious consideration, it is not for me to say. But let us concentrate on this point : that the removal of fear, of quite reasonable fear, is the riddle of the Sphinx. If the League can solve it, it will have succeeded in its work ; if not, it will have failed.

I am hopeful about the purification and elevation of patriotism. Chauvinism or jingoism is, after all, a romantic anachronism. No nation now really desires unwilling subjects ; and in numerous ways the civilised world is being drawn together by new links. Distance is being abolished ; foreign travel, intermarriage, business, sport, the new wonderful means of communication, are all drawing the nations nearer together. " Sirs, ye are brethren ; why do ye wrong one to another ? " We cannot and do not hate foreigners in the concrete. Is it possible that we shall long continue to cherish animosity against abstractions, against symbols like Uncle Sam and John Bull, against this or that flag ? If we are naturally pugnacious we must find some safety valve for that instinct. Sabre-rattling and flag-waving is too dangerous a game to be allowed.

This is a sermon, not a lecture, and a sermon is always addressed to individuals. What can we do, what can you and I do, for peace ? We can put away hatred and vindictiveness from our hearts. We can try to understand the point of view of other nations and to help our countrymen to understand it. We can avoid expecting too much, and yet we can remember that as ice melts at a certain temperature so does the human heart. Without quixotically surrendering important interests, we can look out for opportunities of generous conduct towards foreigners and foreign nations. We can let our diplomatists and statesmen know that the cunning of a smart solicitor outwitting the lawyers on the other side is exactly what we do not want from them.   And, lastly, we can remember the League in our prayers, and bring our earnest desire for peace before Him who is the Prince of Peace.   The knowledge that the same intercessions are rising day by day from men of good will in every nation under heaven will consecrate our endeavours, and increase our faith that God will grant us what we know to be in accordance with His will and what we ardently long for.   May the Holy Spirit guide the counsels of the League and inspire it with wisdom and understanding. Do you remember how in Isaiah the enumeration of the seven gifts of the Spirit is followed immediately by the visions of idyllic peace ?   " The wolf shall dwell with the lamb, and the leopard shall lie down with the kid : and a little child shall lead them."

THE REOPENING OF ST. PAUL'S, JUNE, 1930*

THE metaphor of a building is the one which St. Paul loves best. The vision of the great Christian temple which is the Church, rising day by day upon its eternal foundations, is never far from his mind's eye ; and here he amplifies it. He tells the Corinthians that he himself is the master-builder, chosen by God to lay the foundation on which others are building. The foundation is the only possible one —that which has been laid, even Jesus Christ. That is to say, if a man lays any other foundation, it is not a Christian Church which he is building. But it is possible to build badly on a good foundation ; and sooner or later bad work will be found out. He fears that bad work has been done at Corinth.

Who are the builders ? They are all who try to do any work for God, and the gold, silver, marble, wood, hay, stubble, are the work which they do. The word "edification", which means building, has passed into common speech. There is a slight wavering in the metaphor ; in verses 9 and 17 the Christians themselves are the building ; in verses 10 to 15 their works are the materials out of which the temple is constructed. He does not wish to keep the two apart. The builders bring their own lives to be built up with their works into the sacred building. "Ye are the temple of God." "Know ye not that your bodies are the temples of God ? "

"The day" of which St. Paul speaks is any time of crisis, in which the perishable perishes and the stable remains. The Great War was such a "day" for European civilisation—a

* A Sermon preached in the Cathedral.

day "revealed in fire", fire which proves every man's work of what sort it is. Then the good builder shall receive his due wage, while the bad builder shall lose the fruit of his labour. He himself shall be "saved", inasmuch as he put his hand to the work ; but he will see his unsubstantial walls falling about his ears, and will be glad to escape, naked and homeless, from the blazing pile.

Bad and useless work may be done by sincere Christians. The sight of this is what troubles St. Paul. The brisk competition of the Petrines and Paulines and the disciples of Apollos does not please him, and still less does he like their eagerness to claim credit for their own leaders and to disparage the others. " Are ye not carnal ? " he says. Good work for God cannot be done in this spirit. Ambitious partisanship leads to showy and shoddy production—" walls daubed with untempered mortar," as the Old Testament prophet says. That kind of work will not stand the fire.

We often think that impatient and flimsy work is characteristic of our time. We look at our old churches, and say with Wordsworth, " They thought not of a perishable home, who thus could build." Our new buildings, perhaps fortunately, were not built for eternity. But we need not make too much of this. The Middle Ages expressed themselves naturally in architecture—frozen music, as it has been called. Our age has found other means of self-expression.

A great cathedral like this is not merely a commodious shelter for three or four thousand people who want to listen to music and hear sermons. It is a symbol of the real temple of God, the house not made with hands, eternal in the heavens. It is as grand as the architects and builders could make it, because the Church on earth should show in its outward manifestations that it is a copy of the glorious Church in heaven, not having spot or wrinkle or any such thing, holy and without blemish.

The old builders did not build private houses in this way, unless they were fortified castles. It was only the houses of God which were to stand, if possible, for all time.

We know the history of this splendid pile which now, after five years, has been thrown open in all its pristine majesty. There was another great Cathedral before it on the same site, which perished through no fault of its builders, but by an accident against which they could not provide—the Great Fire of 1666. Old St. Paul's was not entirely destroyed, and there can be no doubt that if the disaster had happened in our own time, the old cathedral would have been exactly restored, as the French have restored the cathedral at Rheims. But in the seventeenth century they thought they could do better than build churches in the Gothic style, and we can hardly regret the decision which gave us Sir Christopher Wren's masterpiece. The fire in point of fact saved us from a horrible hybrid between the two styles.

I spoke of shoddy building—of the wood, hay, stubble which unconscientious builders sometimes bring to the temple of God. We cannot blame Sir Christopher Wren, who was cramped by a niggardly government ; but we know that his great piers under the dome were not solid, and that this defect, after more than two hundred years, has caused us all this trouble, and the great expense which private donors have so generously defrayed. We hope now that all is sound, and that the building may stand secure for centuries.

We reasonably hope so : but mankind is a destructive race. I lately stood among the ruins of the Parthenon at Athens, built in the fifth century before Christ, spared in countless wars, turned into a Christian cathedral and so carefully tended, and then, still intact in all its beauty, blown to pieces by the Venetians only two hundred and fifty years ago. And now that Athens has become a busy and smoky town, the exquisite marble statues on the Acropolis are coming off in flakes, eaten away by the sulphuric acid in the air. The last thirty years have done more damage then the two thousand years before them. We cannot be sure that this cathedral will survive the next war, if (which Heaven avert) there is another war.

When, a week earlier, I stood on the site of Herod's temple at Jerusalem, I recalled our Lord's prediction of its total destruction, though it was then new and imposing enough to excite the admiration of his disciples. And how little it troubled him ! " Destroy this temple, and in three days (that is, in a very short time) I will raise it up." He had brought into the world an enthusiasm which, as he foresaw, would build grander temples than Herod's. It is only when genius has faded and enthusiasm cooled that we think of great works of art as irreplaceable.

And so, amid all our pride and thankfulness to-day, we are drawn to think of this material structure as the product and the temporary habitation of a spirit more indestructible than itself. Old St. Paul's is gone ; new St. Paul's may or may not be standing five hundred years hence. But the spirit of the Church of England, which built the first, which built and has now restored the second, will live as long as its material fabrics and its spiritual temples are founded on a rock firmer than London clay, on the foundation which standeth sure, on Jesus Christ, the same yesterday and to-day and for ever.

Old St. Paul's heard the scholarly eloquence of John Colet, the champion of an intellectual and moral Reformation which was quenched in the flood of the rougher Reformation and the reaction against it which soon followed his death. It was drowned in blood in the hideous Wars of Religion and the atrocities of the Inquisition. But the cause for which he and Erasmus lived is not dead ; it may yet help to transform our traditional Christianity, and to cement an alliance with what is good and true in modern science and humanism. Nor can I forget how Colet, the most illustrious of my predecessors, risked his position and his life by preaching from the pulpit of St. Paul's an earnest and most courageous protest against the unjust war which his formidable master, Henry VIII, was planning against France. Old St. Paul's in the next century heard the splendid discourses of the poet-dean, Donne, an enigmatical figure whose piety in his later years we need not doubt though, like Spenser, he had to confess " Many lewd lays (ah, woe is me the more !) have I in the heat of youth made heretofore." This present building has been ennobled by the refined beauty of Dean Church's sermons and addresses, by the manly directness of Lightfoot, the fervid rhetoric of Liddon, and by the best that many other ornaments of our Church had to give. The Spirit divides to every man severally as he wills. Our national Church, which, please God, shall remain the national Church and no mere sect among other sects, has room for minds of every type, and can use the services of all who love the Lord Jesus Christ in uncorruptness. There is hardly one among all who have helped to shape the life of the Church of England, whether as thinkers, orators, or ecclesiastical administrators and statesmen, who have not at one time or another preached in St. Paul's. Our endeavour now is to invite the best representatives of all schools of thought in the Church, and though the sermon perhaps has not so much power as in the last century, I do not think it has fallen off in quality.

We must not forget the part which the Cathedral took during the Great War, by thanksgiving services, such as the impressive service after America joined the Allies, and the solemn commemoration of the gallant dead belonging to different arms of the service and different portions of the

Empire. On these occasions the unique position of St. Paul's as the central church of the British Commonwealth of Nations was emphasised. The great Reopening Service last week is fresh in our memories. It was a national thanksgiving, in which every branch of the national life was represented. And we were particularly glad to be assured of the sympathy and good-will of other Christian bodies, both at home and abroad.

Next Sunday we look forward to an equally impressive service, when the bishops from the whole Anglican Communion will meet here to ask the blessing of God and the guidance of the Holy Spirit on their deliberations at Lambeth, which we hope will bear good fruit in dealing with the numerous problems, administrative, religious, and moral, which press for solution. Seldom has an assembly more fit to stir the imagination been gathered together. A glance at the map of the world may justify us in thinking that it is as worthy of the name of an Ecumenical Council as any that in former days met at Constantinople or at Rome. The British-speaking nations will be, for once, reunited. The bishops will meet full of questions affecting their own dioceses ; and these are spread over all the five continents, Europe, Asia, Africa, America, and Australasia. That this unique and wonderful Council will inaugurate their sessions by a service under our dome is a thought which may well make us proud and thankful.

But before closing I must return to the symbolic meaning which St. Paul draws out of the material parts of a great temple. St. Peter, you will remember, uses the same figure. Christ Himself is the stone rejected by the builders, but now the head of the corner. And " ye also, as living stones, are built up a spiritual house, to be a holy priesthood, to offer up spiritual sacrifices acceptable to God through Jesus Christ." The design of the building is not our affair. We have just to offer to the Master Builder a bit of honest material—gold, silver, marble—the best we have to give, ourselves and our life's work, in the hope that He may find some place for it in the glorious Temple which is rising day by day and year by year—the invisible Temple of which this great Church of ours is meant to remind us. And St. Paul gives us a terrible warning. "If any man defile the Temple of God, him shall God destroy, for the Temple of God is holy, which Temple ye are." Let us then, before we leave the building this morning, pray that by God's grace we may be able to offer the Divine Architect something which He in His infinite kindness may be able to accept.

MADE AND PRINTED IN GREAT BRITAIN
BY THE BOWERING PRESS, PLYMOUTH